AF457384

Adventures into the Unknown

DD Kosambi, 1907-1966

Adventures into the Unknown

Essays by D D Kosambi

Edited by

Ram Ramaswamy

Jawaharlal Nehru University, New Delhi 110 067

Three Essays
COLLECTIVE

First Edition January 2016

copyright©Ram Ramaswamy and Three Essays Collective 2016
All rights reserved

No part of this book may be reproduced or utilised in any form or by any means, electronic or mechanical, including photocopying, recording or by any information storage or retrieval system, without the prior written permission of the publisher.

ISBN 978-93-83968-11-4

Three Essays
COLLECTIVE
B-957 Palam Vihar, GURGAON (Haryana) 122 017 India
Tel: 91-124 236 9023, +91 98681 26587, +91 98683 44843
info@threeessays.com Website: www.threeessays.com
Printed and bound at Chaman Offset Printers, New Delhi

H.J.B. – Answer required urgently! D.D.K.

Kosambi to Bhabha in the early years at TIFR.
(Courtesy TIFR Archives)

Contents

Preface

Although nearly fifty years have passed since his death in 1966, D. D. Kosambi remains a deeply influential thinker of modern India. His multifaceted intellect led him to contribute in a wide spectrum of areas that ranged from pure mathematics and statistics to history, political theory, numismatics, Indology, epigraphy and linguistics. As a scholar he was prolific, writing nearly 150 articles and essays (about half of which were in mathematics and statistics, the remainder being in other areas), four books and five edited volumes. There is also a large volume of Kosambi's unpublished work that consists of reports, letters, notes, and drafts of essays and articles. In addition, at least two complete manuscripts of his mathematics books are known to have been misplaced or lost.

Of the four essays in this collection two, 'An Introduction to Lectures on Dialectical Materialism' and 'On Statistics' are from among his unpublished papers and notes. The first was written in 1943, and the other probably in the late 1940's or early 1950's. The other two essays have been published earlier.

'Atomic Energy for India' is the transcript of a public talk given by Kosambi in 1960, and the last, the posthumously published autobiographical 'Adventure into the Unknown' was written in the mid 1960's. In the period of nearly a quarter century that these essays span, Kosambi's intellectual life was in ferment, as he moved from mathematics to statistics to numismatics and history, and also increasingly to political positions that caused him considerable friction with his colleagues at the Fergusson College and at the TIFR. During these years he travelled to the USA, to the Soviet Union, and to China, and these excursions influenced his thinking and his attitudes significantly. Together, this quartet offers a glimpse of the didact in Kosambi.

A brief chronology of DDK's professional life may be helpful in situating the four essays in this volume.

1907	Born on July 31 in Goa.
1918–29	Moves to the USA, to Cambridge, Mass., with his father. Studies at the Cambridge Grammar School and Latin High School. Graduates *summa cum laude* from Harvard University and is elected *Phi Beta Kappa*.
1930	Returns to a teaching position in Banaras. Starts publishing independently.
1931	Moves to Aligarh. Publishes in French and German journals.
1933	Moves to Poona to teach mathematics at the Fergusson College.
1939–41	His first publications in areas other than mathematics start appearing.
1945	Joins the Tata Institute of Fundamental Research, Bombay, at the invitation of Homi J. Bhabha.
1956	*Introduction to the Study of Indian History* is published.

1959–62	The years of the Riemann debacle. Is increasingly isolated in TIFR and is essentially ostracised by the mathematics community.
1962	His contract at the Tata Institute of Fundamental Research is not renewed. *Myth and Reality* is published.
1964–66	Appointed Emeritus Professor (of the Council of Scientific and Industrial Research, New Delhi) at the Maharashtra Vidnyanvardhini in Poona. Passes away in his sleep on June 29, 1966. He was not yet 59.

From the ages of 26 to 38, Kosambi was in Poona and teaching at the Fergusson College, not always happily. Nevertheless, he was in an intensely creative period of his life. In 1935, he was awarded the Ramanujan Medal of the Madras University and was elected to the Indian Academy of Sciences, Bangalore. He was asking original questions of a mathematical nature and corresponding with leading mathematicians in France and elsewhere. During these years, he was to devote considerable effort to the study of what he termed *path-geometry* in mathematics. His interest in statistics led to his work in numismatics (starting in 1940) and eventually to the important papers on proper orthogonal decomposition (in 1942 and 1943). On the way, he wrote a paper that was critical of the Zipf analysis in linguistics (in 1942), and made the contribution that has kept his name alive in genetics as the Kosambi distance (1944). The most intellectually fertile period of Kosambi's Poona years coincided with World War II, when he wrote most of the papers that constitute the bulk of his mathematical legacy.[1]

1 A complete bibliography and copies of all DDK's papers became available only in 2013. This is now available in the Open Access Repository of publications of Fellows of the Indian Academy of Sciences, Bangalore, http://www.ias.ac.in

This was the time when his reputation in areas other than mathematics grew. His careful analysis of coin-weights caught the attention of historians. He taught himself Sanskrit well enough to publish a scholarly commentary on the poetry of Bhartrhari. But also in 1943 (when he was just about 36 years old) he decided to give a course of lectures on Marxism to the citizens of Poona. The prècis of his lectures survives as 'An Introduction To Lectures On Dialectical Materialism'. This essay, which may have been annotated later, is remarkable for its content and given the range of Kosambi's interests, it is admirable that he not only gave this set of lectures, but that he also found the time to write out detailed notes.

By 1945, DDK had moved to the TIFR on the invitation of the Director, Homi Bhabha, to help set up the School of Mathematics. Their relationship was very cordial in the initial years, as the letters and notes in the TIFR archives testify. DDK appears to have participated in the ongoing research and he mentored some students at that time, writing joint papers with two of them on problems of a statistical nature. These were, respectively, with S. Raghavachari on seasonal variations on the Indian birth-and death-rates (in 1951 and 1954), and with U. V. Ramamohan Rao on the efficiency of randomization by card-shuffling (somewhat later, in 1958). The second essay, On Statistics appears to date from this time and may have been given as a lecture at Bombay House (which even today is the headquarters of the Tata Group of companies). There is not much formal statistics in the article (indeed there is not a single equation) but the fairly discursive and mildly polemical tone reflects the mixture of ideas that were basic to Kosambi's thinking. Some of Kosambi's "Marxist way of seeing things" also appealed to Homi Bhabha then, as noted by Robert Anderson.[2]

---

2 *Nucleus and Nation: Scientists, International Networks, and Power in*

But from the mid-1950's, there was increasingly a clash of styles and values between Kosambi on the one hand and Bhabha and the TIFR establishment on the other. *Introduction to the Study of Indian History* secured Kosambi's position as a major thinker and historian, and his lack of investment and engagement in the TIFR School of Mathematics led to his professional marginalization as a mathematician. Indeed, although he continued to publish, his work was of limited interest to his colleagues, and the resulting intellectual isolation led him to make a disastrous error. He published a paper that claimed a result that would prove the most celebrated (and still unproven) hypothesis in all of mathematics.[3] By the end of the 1950's, Kosambi's continuance in the TIFR was in jeopardy: the mathematical *faux pas* aside, his strong views against the use of nuclear energy were in direct conflict with the Department of Atomic Energy, the parent organization that funded the TIFR.

The third essay 'Atomic Energy for India' is the text of a talk given by DDK to the Rotary Club of Poona in 1960. Although this essay has appeared earlier in various collections, the basic message of Kosambi, that solar energy held more promise for a developing nation like India compared to atomic energy that was being promoted aggressively. At the time the talk was given, DDK 's differences with Bhabha were out in the open, and the differences were not just in politics. They were there in practical issues such as the estimation of risks, on matters of distribution, of the pattern of investment in research, and a major difference in their perception of India. What DDK said then, that "*Solar energy is not something that any villager*

India, R. S. Anderson, Chicago University Press, 2010.

3 See *e.g.* R. Ramaswamy, *A scholar in his time: Contemporary views of Kosambi the mathematician*, Occasional Paper of the Nehru Memorial Museum and Library, Perspectives in Indian Development, New Series 45 (2014).

can convert for use with his own unaided efforts, at a negligible personal expenditure, charkha style. It means good science and first-rate technology whose results must be made available to the individual user" was only too true: it has taken over fifty years, but today, as India, like much of the world turns to solar energy for our power requirements, this is a good essay to read afresh. Three Mile Island, Chernobyl and Fukushima have played their role in educating the public at large on the risks imposed by large atomic reactors, and it is instructive to recall DDK's early and very passionate espousal of small-scale decentralized solar energy units for India. The essence of his arguments still remain valid, even as the world has changed and India has changed so drastically since then.

The final essay in this collection is an autobiographical note that was published posthumously in 1972 in Current Trends in Indian Philosophy edited by K. Satchidananda Murty and K. Ramakrishna Rao[4] wherein he reflects on his "personal philosophy as a scientist and research worker". An excerpted and bowdlerized version of this article was published as "Steps in Science" in the collection *Science and Human Progress*.[5] Both manifesto and autobiography, 'Adventure into the Unknown' offers a rare and frank glimpse into the inner workings of a gifted mind. The final section, the Epilogue does not appear in the more widely circulated "Steps in Science". Although short, the last part of this essay makes it amply clear that Kosambi was well aware of the shortcomings of his flawed mathematical approach to the Riemann hypothesis.

The four essays are presented here in the order in which they were written. They display a side of D. D. Kosambi that is not always apparent in other writings on or by him, that of

---

4 Asia Publishing House, Bombay, 1972.

5 *Science and Human Progress: Essays in honour of late Prof. D. D. Kosambi, scientist, Indologist, and humanist*, Popular Prakashan, Mumbai, 1974.

a pedagogue. His desire to communicate the essence of the Marxist method, or of Statistics, and his ability to draw examples and analogies from a vast cultural canvas make these essays speak across the gap of more than fifty years. The passion of his advocacy of solar energy, and the simplicity and directness of his arguments for a distributed and decentralized approach to energy make Kosambi appear more than prescient: these same principles guide many public policies at the current time. It is a matter of great regret that he was not taken seriously, and more that his personal angularities and his intellectual isolation resulted in his good ideas not gaining currency when it was necessary.

The last essay lends its name to this collection very naturally. The first two essays were largely unknown; even though they were in typescript, the manuscripts were not very widely circulated, and in any case never published elsewhere. DDK could not have known just how right he would be about the importance of solar energy in 1960; much of that talk was based on speculation and intelligent extrapolation in an unknown direction.

Kosambi's personal philosophy and ethos is etched clearly in the final essay's Epilogue. He considered himself a mathematician, first and last. Along the way he was many other things, but of the value of his contributions he had unforgiving standards. In the fifty years since he died, though, it is clear that he was probably harsher on himself than he need have been, and he was probably harsher on himself than he was on others. His contributions have survived, not just in the many areas that he touched, such as "statistics, Indology, archaeology and the rest", but also in the area that he valued the most, in mathematics.

I was fortunate to have met Meera Kosambi in 2010 when I started to put together a complete bibliography of D. D. Kosambi's mathematical œuvre. On finding that the lists that existed then were incomplete in one way or the other, I asked for help in the hope that some author's reprint copies might be remaining among his personal papers. As it happened, in the course of searching for them, she did allow me to rifle through some box of papers and letters. The first two essays were "discovered" in this manner, and the idea of this book was born then, with her enthusiastic support. She also allowed me to take copies of personal photographs for use in the book. It is a matter of great personal regret that she did not live to see it completed.

Ram Ramaswamy
New Delhi, January 2016

Chapter 1

An Introduction to Lectures on Dialectical Materialism

This set of notes form a commentary used with fifteen lectures that I gave by invitation between the dates of April 15 and May 9, 1943. The main purpose of the lectures was to introduce the audience to the philosophy called dialectical materialism, or after its founder, Marxism. This was done, insofar as the time allotted to me and my own capacities permitted, by a rapid reading of Lenin's *Teachings of Karl Marx* and *The Communist Manifesto*. It would have been most pleasing to add the positive sections of Engels' *Anti-Dühring*, but the time was certainly not enough for this extra portion. The present rather scrappy notes helped introduce the students while their reading was under way and they helped me learn the subject for myself, for I am certainly not an adept or an initiate, having myself to think out each development of the subject slowly and painfully. In any case, the notes, though laying no claim to originality, are intended to persuade the reader, if not to prove to him, that Marxism is a tool that can be applied to problems which present themselves every day in India as in other countries.

No tool can work of its own accord; the dexterity with which one wields it depends upon one's own practice, application, industry, and intelligence, both in the choice of material and in it's shaping. So with Marxism, a tool of analysis inasmuch as it is a new way of thinking, it will first be necessary for the user to have or to acquire the habit of thinking for himself. He will, in addition, have to find material to which to apply that tool from his own observation, experience, reading. Otherwise his acquisition will remain, like much of the education of our universities and colleges, an empty discipline, a minor pastime, an inoculation against the disease of original thought.

I do not claim to be an authority on Marxism, nor to set myself up against those who, even in India, have given vent to authoritative utterances. Several have inveighed against Marxism without taking the trouble to study it, simply because it means "the importation of foreign ideas into India". But these persons invariably speak in English, a foreign language, dress in clothes of a foreign cut, probably of foreign material purchased to show their capacity for conspicuous consumption, hold some such foreign honour as a knighthood [how it would have astonished the company that sat at good King Arthur's Round Table to see what history had in store for their order] from a foreign government, and still quest after the receding Grail of further gain from foreign masters or from a foreign mode of production, shares, factories and such. So it seems clear that these worthies objected more to ideas as such than to anything foreign. With them and their descending trailers of parasites I have no bone to pick; they control Indian education and have succeeded only too well in stamping out all ideas in order to keep away the dangerous ones.

More serious are the parties (at least three of them when enough members are found outside the jails) that profess some variety of Marxism in India, or claim individually to have better interpretations of Marx than any other. It would have been worthwhile to criticise each of their ideologies and that of the Indian National Congress [whenever it is possible to distill any ideology at all from their publications and reported speeches], had it not been giving a tool to the vigorous forces of reaction. All I can advise any student to do is to go to the best teachers of Marxism: Marx himself, followed by Engels, Lenin and Stalin. To appreciate their work, in all its depth and power, it is essential to grasp the facts of the situations with which they dealt, the historical background which they took for granted. This was the hardest part of my task in giving (spoken) commentaries on the reading matter. To one who has learned European history in an Indian educational institution, even the first paragraph of the *Communist Manifesto* is incomprehensible. Patricians and plebeians, guildmasters and journeymen, lords and serfs are all equally beyond his mental horizon. Yet, properly directed, these matters would be easier for an Indian to understand than for any European. He who lives in a country where a *gotra* is still a living reality can understand without much effort the nature of the gentilic and the patriarchal society most Indians are brought up, as I was myself, in households which are slight modifications of the ancient patriarchal forms. The duties and obligations of a feudal lordling may still be observed in the more backward portions of the country, though it is far easier to see how the older forms of property are being converted under British law into modern capitalistic property, how mere accumulation, still to be seen everywhere, turns more and more rapidly into capital under the pressure of modern life, legislation, taxation, and more particularly of modern war. Every form of society, from the neolithic or heliolithic tribes that that pushed their way into Chota Nagpur from the northeast perhaps as late as the fourth century A.D. to the most modern associations of capitalist exploiters are to be observed in India. Not in their original form, nor static and insulated from newer currents, but interacting, forming a rapidly shifting cultural pattern, rather a complicated set of overlapping patterns that would form the most fascinating material for any student. Unfortunately – and as every Marxist will see, quite naturally – there are no students interested in the problem of studying this situation as a whole. The Western mechanism of scientific study is blunted in our hands to a crude toy for producing the feeblest of memoirs and papers, for grubbing a few allowances and grants; every year, our intelligentsia hears someone of its members propose that they should all gather together to make a new Renaissance. Unfortunately, renaissances are not "made" in this fashion, they have to bloom as the expression of a new form of society, one far more productive and kinder to its members than the older one; if any member of our intelligentsia should try to realise this and to bring it about, however, he is apt to find himself looking at the world from behind the thick bars of a jail. Communism is now safe to profess, almost a fashion; have I not heard an Anglo-Indian police official proclaim openly that he was a communist, and therefore convinced that India had about the best possible system of government, though it needed younger blood (about his own age) to administer it properly.

But hard study has not been a fashion involved more than mugging up set texts for an examination Otherwise, those who wanted to study Marxism would find enormous stores of untouched materials ready to be worked over, and would also see the changes predicted by Marx and Engels take place with scientific regularity.

Lecture 1

At the outset let us define two terms which appear throughout any course on Marxism, and which are usually misunderstood in any bourgeois society. Our popular conception of an *idealist* is that of a noble, somewhat unpractical personage who professes the highest ideals and is willing, if necessary, to suffer for them; a *materialist* is taken to be the contrary type, the shabby fellow who looks for base gain on all occasions, These are *not* the meanings we attach to these terms in what follows. *Idealism* is the philosophy professed by an idealist is always to be taken to mean the attitude that matter exists only as a reflection of our ideas and concepts thereof, having no independent existence, reality has no other meaning to the idealist beyond this faith in his own mental processes. *Materialism*, on the contrary, maintains that matter exists prior to and independently of our own cognition of it, our sensations, ideas, concepts are themselves extensions of matter, the reaction of matter by its interaction wit our bodies, our nervous system, brain – all themselves material. No extra-material process is involved in the action of what we may choose to call the mind, the soul, the spirit, or any similar term.

This formulation of materialism is the basic postulate of dialectical materi-alism. We shall take it as our fundamental postulate without further argument. Note that in India, the idealist view is completely ingrained, not only in the immense accumulation of religious philosophy, but in the language itself. The Sanskrit word *padārtha* is literally "word-meaning", though it denotes "material object". So, it is natural for the average Indian to assume, without a conscious effort on his part to the contrary, that objects are word-meanings, reflections of the words he makes up, of his ideas. The Chinese, though their means of production are similar to ours and though the social similarity is quite profound, think differently in these matters; even today, in spite of the vast tomes of Indian [particularly Buddhistic] philosophy translated into Chinese, the modern Chinese finds it hard to grasp certain Indian ways of expression and very difficult indeed to translate some of Mahatma Gandhi's utterances.

The harassed student may exclaim, "What does it matter if the structure of our language is topsy-turvy? After all, whether we say that the world goes around the sun or the sun around the world, we face the same facts of regular sunrise and sunset. Why then quibble about materialism and idealism? This "quibble" becomes of the utmost importance on the social level. Theories of the solar system and of cosmogony can at most delay or advance scientific progress, but on the social level, people tend to justify their form of production by their theories: to impose their ideas upon reality. The reactionary grasps the fundamental importance of basic notions far better than most amateur revolutionaries. Thus, when people were dealt with by the Holy Inquisition for challenging the cosmogony or the anatomical notions founded upon Aristotle – after a careful revision by patristic scholars – it was really because these intellectual rebels were breaching the complete wall of a given social philosophy and structure, and the flood was sure to pour in. It is not true to say that society adjusted itself to these new discoveries, that the Church remained undamaged by them, it was an altogether different form of society that needed these new discoveries, a totally new Protestant church developed while the Catholic church readjusted itself so slowly as to survive with the greatest loss of power and prestige. The perversions of the terms idealism and materialism with which this section opens are also a clever attempt on the part of the classes in possession of property and production, therefore of education, to strangle new thought. Here it is of prime importance to realize that ideas are developed as an expression of productive forms, and that the converse view is fatal.

Lecture 2

Dialectical materialism takes a very important step beyond materialism in setting down some fundamental laws deduced from the observation of matter and material processes. These "laws" are not to be taken as immutable dogmas, though we shall set them down also as postulates, to save time. They have been deduced and tested, utilized for further experimental work and prediction, modified and extended as need arose, just like any other scientific laws. The dialectical process consists of three stages: thesis, antithesis, synthesis. The thesis is the initial stage with which we start. This stage cannot remain immutably fixed, no existence is possible without change; change, including motion [= change of position] is the mode of existence of matter. You might note that this is a fundamental tenet of Buddhist and some pre-Buddhist philosophies, as well as of Marxism. But Marxism, developing the Hegelian dialectic, maintains that change inherent in the thesis, in the initial state of any material aggregate, leads to the negation of that state, its antithesis, its diametrical opposite. But the process cannot terminate there, it must continue as it has begun so that this opposite, this antithesis) is also negated – the negation of the negation. By the ordinary rules of grammar, this should lead to the original state; not so in dialectic philosophy. The synthesis, the negation of the negation, only brings you parallel to the initial position, but always on a different level. You have not gone around in a circle, but in a spiral. History never repeats itself; there is always a difference of level between any two stages however similar. We have the thermodynamical principle that entropy must always increase, so that processes involving matter with transfer of heat are irreversible. This is true with far greater force on the social level. Hitler may profess the rugged ideals of the Stone Age, but he cannot go back to its tools, to the Stone Age means of production. The charkhā of Mahātmā

Gāndhī can be a most potent political weapon against foreign bourgeois exploiters but it can never displace Indian mills except by an inconceivable use of violence on an unprecedented scale, and even then for not more than a short time.

To visualise the process, think of the filament of the coiled-coil electric bulbs [unfortunately so rare these days! But here I have a piece of ordinary wire with which I actually construct the model described]. The original filament is first wound in a small spiral, then this spiral coiled upon itself. Suppose you had a second spiral made thus, then coiled that into a third bigger one and so on. If you looked at the whole masse from a distance, it would appear to be a small ball of wire inextricably tangled. If you could, like some minute insect, take up a position on the wire you will find it possible to crawl along, but impossible to say where the ultimate position would be. In fact, the question of goal is, with a wire of indefinite length, quite meaningless for the crawling insect. The continuity and the possibility of progress are both there, the bewildered insect as well as the distant observer who would round out the whole mass as a small tangled ball of wire are both wrong in their interpretation.[1]

On the social level, the question of ultimate aims can be raised and such aims laid down only by idealists. We can see far enough ahead in the present form of society to say what its negation ought to be, but with fresh productive forms will come fresh knowledge, will appear new goals, better means of realization. One other point is to be noted, that of size and scale. Progress is otherwise a meaningless term. (One man's death does not terminate society, though "progress" for him is ended). Some states might even seem to regress to the point of extinction, as in Mesopotamia; these may be compared to

1 DDK's handwritten annotation: Spirals, one inside the other lead, in the limit, to concepts like Weierstrass' non-differentiable function, the wire having continuity but no direction at any point.

the dinosaurs and to the extinct forms of man: *Sinathropus*, the Java, Piltdown, Heidelberg, Cromagnards and other specimens, equally extinct dead ends of evolutionary processes. Your wire spiral has split off like the bypath of a maze and terminated so that there is no inevitability of progress for a selected group.

But humanity has evolved, has gone on to more efficient and productive social forms. It might be as well to state here that progress is an abstraction that does not often mean the same thing to all speakers. The Romans were considered by most historians to have been ahead of the people that followed; that may be justified after a fashion for the people who inhabited the geographical site of the ancient city during the middle ages. For Europe as a whole, the medieval and even the feudal period was unquestionably one of progress; not progress from the point of view of the archaeologist who is far more impressed with the remnants of Nero's *domus aurea* than with the idea of millions of hovels that have vanished – but for society as a whole, the middle ages meant the evolution of more productive and more tolerable forms and relationships. You must not judge civilisation only by the comparison of classical poetry with medieval palimpsests. Ask yourselves whether or not more people had roofs over their heads, had clothes made of wool and linen in place of leather, had more metal to work with, could defend themselves better against disease and contemporary invaders, and so on. Then progress will take on a different meaning.

Lecture 3

There is one further important law that you will find essential for any Marxist analysis. We saw the continuity of the spiral, but this is not uniform. There are changes so rapid as to seem discontinuous, cataclysmic at times. These come under the third postulate: *mere change of quantity must ultimately lead to a change of quality*. The classical example of this is the change of water by cooling [loss of quantity of heat] into ice; or by heating into steam. In each case we may proceed by adding heat or taking it away at a quite steady rate, but there will come a time of abrupt change of state in the substance. Marxism postulates that this is inevitable.

The nature of the inevitability is in itself an illustration of the dialectic process and of the further law, that the *properties of matter are inexhaustible*. We know now that there is not one but that there are several different kinds of ice, with different physical properties as you go down the scale of temperature; also, if you heat steam enormously, the structure changes far beyond that of simple water vapour and at temperatures that prevail in the sun or the hotter stars, you would find it very difficult to recognize any water vapour – sometime even the constituent gases hydrogen and oxygen become difficult to recognize. So, we see that in a single quantitative chain there may be many changes of quality. Some of these might also be very close together.

There is more to the dialectics of change than just this, however. A simple statement about the change is, due to the inexhaustible properties of matter, a great simplification of an unending series of complicated steps within. The dialectic process itself applies to the determination of the point where the change takes place, the critical or threshold value of physicists and biologists. As soon as this value is approached, other factors that seemed of no importance arise and claim the observer's attention. Ice may be converted directly into steam without passing through the intermediate stage of water, if you adjust the pressure and temperature properly. When we say that water will change into ice at 0° Centigrade, we assume a certain pressure, a standard of purity, and today a definite low proportion of heavy hydrogen in the constituent gas. But even apart from this, as will be seen from the certainty of other conditions becoming known later on, the statement is true only in a statistical manner, the result given is on the basis of a large number of observations under the set conditions, the unknown factors cancelling out in the long run on the whole. For example, we can, with very careful laboratory technique, cool water to below 0° without changing the pressure and without changing it into ice simply because the first ice crystal was not allowed to form. This can be seen far better in salt solutions which have a known point of saturation above which crystallization must generally take place. But supersaturated solutions can be made, and the change to the solid state takes place in the twinkling of an eye if some impurity or a parent crystal is added. That is why so many of the hydrocarbons that our chemists make are very difficult to crystallize for the first time. The parent crystal, in many substances, determines the shape of the crystals in the mass, because it is also possible for the entire substance to exist in several different crystalline forms.

What we can say in a statement of this sort is that for every change of state there are in reality *two* threshold values: one below which the change an cannot take place, and one above which the change must take place. In between, the exact point of change is indeterminate because other conditions, hitherto unimportant, become of prime importance. Inevitability is not mechanical nor fatalistic. This might be kept in mind by those who say that a change of social state is inevitable, so why attempt to bring one about? Make the best of both states and enjoy life. The answer is, no! Change is not inevitable in the same way as water into ice, because we have not been able to observe thousand upon thousands of essentially identical societies in transition, leadership has a very essential role to play in between the two threshold levels of production if a change of state is to be brought about.

Lecture 4

Let us take a few examples to clarify our position. According to Engels in his study of the origins of the family, state etc., primitive society began on a level of communism, common ownership of whatever there was to be owned, each giving to the community according to his ability and taking from it according to his needs. That all societies went through this stage is contested, and certainly the evidence both ways is rather meager, but there is no doubt that at the beginning many societies did so function while others may have taken directly to later forms – just as the industrial revolution in India does not start with the machinery that England developed in changing from feudalism, but takes

to the best machinery available for its money today. Now when the primitive population reached a certain level, increased production became necessary, the environment could not be exploited successfully by the primitive organization of society; so we get the family, the classes of society, the state developing out of earlier units; we get in loose succession the patriarchal, the feudal, the medieval pseudo-capitalist, and the modern machine-manufacturing capitalist societies. Some of these stages run parallel to previous ones, some outrun their productive bases as in Sumeria and to a lesser extent Greece. Many attempt a conscious imitation of their grandparents without success unless they atrophy rapidly. There are some minor repetitions, some portions that run out to extinction. Throughout, we see the modes of thinking change: *man is conditioned by his means of production*. In places where the change is very much slower, as in China and India, because nature was more bountiful and human effort less necessary, a stability is achieved wherein the successive cycles do not emerge on noticeably higher levels, but even these "unchanging" societies must crumble before newer and more efficient means of production. Society as a whole has been going ahead, though not without loss to older forms, not without misery to human beings that constituted the society. What is the end of this spiral of productive spirals, the succession of changes of state caused by an increase of production [including production of human beings in effective social contact]? It must ultimately be another type of communistic society in which each gives according to his ability and takes according to his needs; the classless society must return, but not on the primitive level of production and helplessness before the phenomena of nature. The new level will be far more efficient, a higher level. There is a minimum level of production below which the change to this classless society is impossible, a maximum but unspecifiable level above which the change must necessarily take place. The gap in between, as we see today, is filled with the violence of war, the misery of artificial man-made famine, avoidable pestilence and distress for humanity. The actual transition depends not merely on volume and distribution of production, but upon the subsidiary conditions such as leadership. If the leadership can recognize the attainment of a threshold value and act accordingly, persuading a sufficiently large portion of the working class to participate in that action, the change will take place even with limited resources. This, for example was the great achievement of Lenin, the supreme realist of our times, in completing a gigantic step towards communism when it was not expected to succeed in a backward country like the Tsarist Russia. The existence of a beaten army faced by the war-weary armies of other countries, the existence of an active and advanced proletarian class in a few centers followed by the peasant workers activated by the misery of war had in fact, made it possible to carry the revolution to a stage beyond all previous revolutions. The Soviet Union went from a bourgeois revolution in February to a proletarian dictatorship in October, its leaders saw that the proletarianization of the country, socialization of the means of production had necessarily to be completed at whatever cost, if the new forms were to survive. And if their efforts have certainly not carried them to the ultimate stage, one can assert with equal certainty that they are well on the way, far ahead of any other country. The classless society might have been easier to establish had the revolution succeeded in a more productive country like Germany, but the leadership in all the non-Russian revolutions after 1918 went over to or was wrecked by the owning classes, and stifled the birth of any proletarian dictatorship. This too is an act of leadership, albeit in favour of the class that will fight new developments; Kautsky is the best example here, but you will find plenty of others including Ramsay Macdonald.

What lies beyond that "ultimate" but already visible communistic stage? Are we to reach the stagnation of a human antheap? Degeneration into the sensualists' warren of Mr. Aldous Huxley's "Brave New World"? No! Marx only said that we cannot, at present, see further, that human history will then begin. The spiral passes beyond the vision of even our furthest-sighted analysts. Let us only pause for a moment to consider the objections of those who say that society must necessarily lapse into barbarism because the state, the mechanism of class violence, will wither away, and there will be no method of compelling people to work. This theory, that mankind is too lazy to try for its own survival unless forced to work for the benefit of a few people forming the class in possession has another polar consequence: that the ornament of humanity is the idle class that has not to work, that has only to consume, that has leisure, no matter how acquired. The two, which contradict themselves when placed side by side are intimately connected and separately presented! The forcing of one large class to work for a minority might have been the quickest way of increasing production in older times, but the problem now is of doing something useful with what society produces. Those of you who saw millions of acres of cotton ploughed under when so many millions of people had to go half-naked, that saw thousands of tons of wheat burned in America while millions in this country and China hardly knew what it was to eat a full meal, shiploads of oranges dumped into the bay of Biscay with rachitic British working class children badly in need of vitamins, mountains of Brazilian coffee destroyed to keep prices up you won't have to be convinced that forcing people to work for those who don't know how to distribute the products is the great problem of society. We shall, we must, rise to communism and to a social form far superior to the best now imaginable.

Lecture 5

Let me take a few more examples to drive these points home. The idea of threshold values is exemplified in a way that all of you can understand by considering the wage problem in Poona. As most of you don't know as yet the difference between a proletarian and any poor man, take the example of a household servant who works for wages. No matter how little work you extract from him, you will have to pay him a certain minimum wage, that which his surroundings and his preconceptions of necessity [which derive from his social origins and environment, not from his "ideas"] enables him to regard as the least for subsistence, or he must get that money from other sources, whether he works for the extras or steals them. At the upper threshold, no matter how much you pay him, he will be able to do no more than a certain maximum of work, being a biological organism with a limited output of energy. In between, the better you pay the more you can extract from the worker, on the principle of competition if you like.

The proletarian who works in the factory differs from your servant and from the peasant who tills the land. The servant may hope to become a master some day if he can save, learn, get a better job or inherit something as a reward of faithful services; the peasant can always hope to buy a plot of land for himself, and so become his own and a few other people's master – even though statistics will tell him (in case he wanted to know) that there isn't land enough for him and his fellows too. The proletarian is a person who has nothing to sell except his bodily labour, and cannot possibly hope to purchase a share in the means of production. No worker says to himself "I shall save till the day I can buy a portion of this steam hammer, and so on till I set up a factory of my own". In an *expanding* period of capitalism, such as that which was closed in the USA in 1929, workers could rise by their ability to posts of command, to ownership. There are many American millionaires today who rose from the workbench, the best modern example being that of Chrysler, the motor car producer. But in periods of stability, as in England after 1815, no such rise is possible in numbers large enough to give the proletarian any hope. In India, where the capitalist apparatus comes full-grown from the outside, there is even less hope for the worker, who comes from the land and turns within a few years into a proletarian. The apparatus of exploitation is complete, but the proletariat hasn't grown in proportion; we have a bourgeoisie that sprang full grown from the brains that fed on primitive accumulation, but the proletariat has yet to be created in great contrast to those countries where the bourgeoisie had to develop its own proletariat before being able to make any progress. Every analysis of the Indian and the Chinese situation will have to bear this in mind.

Modern capital has enabled India to jump so far ahead by introducing the vital factor of power; the former position of the human body as the main source of energy is now abolished. The worker's labour power is tremendously enhanced by the machinery which he commands. The purpose of exploitation is, then, to extract the maximum output for as low a wage as possible, to induce the worker to produce near the upper threshold while paying him near the lower one, of his own subsistence; in the meanwhile, his productivity and the rate of exploitation go up with the efficiency of the machine to which he is hitched. The latent contradiction here lies in that ultimately, the producer cannot sell his goods at a profit, because if the system if sufficiently widespread, the purchasing power of the greater part of the population is derived from the wages earned by the proletarians, and so the system must collapse. Thus, in England during 1930–1939, there were many workers with nice savings-bank accounts, but very many more on the dole. The system survived partly by living on its own accumulated fat [which appeared as the dole to workers from other workers' production], partly by colonial exploitation – which we felt and continue to feel so bitterly.

This Marxist deduction is vigorously contested by economists of the classical school, who regard Marxism as exploded because Marx's prophecies according to them – have failed. The condition of the workers has in reality improved steadily under capitalism, hence because of the benevolence of capitalists. The flaw is evident when you study the workers of the world as a whole, apart from the trifling alleviation introduced by expansion of capitalist exploitation into regions where more primitive forms existed. No improvement in the workers' conditions of life came because of capitalist benevolence. Every improvement had to be fought for by mass action of the workers on a sufficiently large scale. When the victory was won, in one corner, for shorter hours, better conditions of work, the defeated capitalists turned about to force legislation through their state apparatus which would bring to rest of the exploiters the same conditions of competition. This explains why the workers conditions are ameliorated by legislation fully controlled by capitalists. Often, the divisions among the capitalists themselves work to the benefit of the proletarians. Lord Shaftesbury, the workers' friend, improved factory conditions and wages, prevented child labour in factories, but he didn't pay his own agricultural labourers anything like decent wages. So, we find the apparent paradox that most radical and democratic legislation in England is passed by the Tory party on occasion as a political weapon in yielding gracefully to the inevitable, and even oftener as a sub-class measure against the more efficient exploiters.

The improvements are not only based in the final analysis upon the workers' powers of organization and threat of mass action, but they are transient. No surplus piled up by the workers can compare with the sufferings during a crisis. These crises are inherent in the capitalist system of production, and crisis here includes the modern capitalist imperialist war between fully developed nations. The brunt of these must necessarily be borne by the workers, whether in unemployment, longer hours of work ["for the national emergency"] higher prices, worse conditions of subsistence, or in the trenches of the battlefields. Official and orthodox economists find it easiest to ignore the crises altogether, or to offer some palliatives, each his own. At best they take the form of the late President Roosevelt's New Deal "pump-priming", (Keynes' panacea for ailing capitalism) expenditure upon public works to stimulate production. This stimulus, if at all successful, usually makes capitalism even more efficient, with more strength to bring about the next crisis. We can see that expenditure in public works was the favourite method in Roman times (as also in Asia) of returning accumulation to circulation. That was the function of acqueducts, bridges, and temples or churches. It left a series of cultural strata, but no end was made to recurring periods of distress because no change occurred in the means of production. So also for modern capital. The fundamental contradiction is between carefully organised production within the factory, social production, as contrasted with individualistic and anarchical methods in the mechanism of distribution. This is not to be solved by priming the pump, but needs a revolution. The medical analogy is that of cancer cells, which proliferate without limit, set up their colonies in all parts of the body, can perform no vital function, but claim the very first and greatest share of the body's nutrition, destroying the entire body unless excised or killed by radiation. Cancer is undirected growth and that is about all we know of it today, as the bulk of human energy has to be canalized towards killing men, not saving them. It staggers the imagination however, knowing what we do now about capitalism, to see bourgeois authors, particularly our economists compare Bolshevism with cancer, planned economy with a disease; it is as if the cancerous growth were to proclaim itself the most important part of the human organism. Only one thing can be said for capital-ism which cannot be said of cancer [to the best of our knowledge today], that it had at one stage of development a function to perform in changing means of production; but that stage is long past, what remains is the deadliness of a carcinoma which monopolizes more and more the nourishment needed for the body.

Lecture 6

I take two examples of Marxist phenomena in science just to show that Marxism is not confined to the simplest of known facts, that it applies to quite complicated theories and discoveries. Dr. B. Ramaswami, working at Bangalore in 1935 coated plates of glass with thin layers of silver by the process of evaporating a silver globule [which could be done by the sudden application of heat in a confined space]. To everyone's surprise the silver film did not fade out gradually towards the edges. In the center, there was a bright mirror-like patch which suddenly changed colour to a greenish band when the film became thin enough, around this was another sudden change to a thinner brownish band, which faded away to irregular and indistinct patches. The central mirror had comparatively low electric resistance, the first band around the mirror had resistance that jumped up to about a hundred times the central value, and the resistance in the outermost detectable band gave another sudden jump. The results puzzled the experimenter till he worked out the structure of the molecular deposit; but it seemed natural enough to the Marxist to whom he was showing the experiment. On the other hand, mere dialectics could never have taken the place of the crucial experiment, nor of the technique; previous methods of coating with silver film were by sputtering, and the results gave nothing like this. Only measurements of the most accurate sort, whether made by a Marxist or not could say where and at what threshold values the sudden changes of state take place.

K. S. Krishnan working systematically years earlier on the absorption spectra of hydrocarbons got to the three and four ring substances like naphthalene and anthracene. Certain of the spectra were found to be due not to the pure substance, but to the presence of minute impurities. The impurities tested by themselves did not give the peculiar spectrum. It was even more puzzling to find that a reasonable mixture of the two also showed nothing more than would be expected from an ordinary mixture. Only when the lower threshold value of the contaminating substance was passed, when the contaminant occurred in such small quantities that its crystals could not take their own shape but had necessarily to orient themselves on the surfaces of the main substance, did one get the peculiarities revealed by the spectroscope; they were due to the fact that a substance had been made to take on a physical form which its molecular structure would not normally have permitted. The experimenter was justly congratulated on a brilliant and difficult piece of research.

Lecture 7

Change of quality with quantity has been seen in medicine, where minute doses of poisons sometimes act as remedies and most drugs in overdoses have a deadly effect. Curare, the deadly vegetable poison of the South American Indians works in the blood stream by paralysing the ends of the nerve fibres, which control voluntary muscle movements; the poisoned animal cannot breathe, eventually suffocating to death. This mechanism of its action was traced by the very beautiful experiments of the great French physiologist Claude Benard who made a tool for exploration of the body out of this most deadly substance. Modern doctors went to the jungle to learn the principles of manufacture; they use curare in very minute doses to relieve pain and facilitate recovery. You have all had some injection of a vaccine or of a serum. The first gives you some dead and sterilized bacilli to digest, the second is from some animal whose blood has changed after digesting the bacillus or the toxin of some disease. Both protect you against the disease and are used for immunization or for cure as the case may be. So we have learned from the capital work of Pasteur that certain bacilli may be used to immunize against the disease that they cause. Note that this doesn't work with all, and that this is not the only or even the best method. Most epidemics are unnecessary; in India they are an infliction upon the people that might easily have been prevented. You have, most of you, had an inoculation against the bubonic plague which visits Poona periodically; the recurrent epidemic can be wiped out altogether with cleaner, less crowded houses. In fact the position now is that those who live in the better houses and cleaner localities are just those rich and educated enough to have themselves protected by an inoculation; the poorer inhabitants are also the dirtier, the more ignorant, the more exposed to infection – they are just the people who are afraid of the hypodermic needle and dodge inoculation, thus keeping the plague going. I know from personal experience that their fear can be overcome, provided you have time and patience enough to gain their confidence, but in fact they form a separate nation, the exploited, by contrast with the "upper" classes who complain of foreign exploitation. Ignorance and poverty combine to form a constant pool of disease. About Poona we have two endemic diseases: Malaria in the river valley to the south, and dracontiasis in the north. Both could be stamped out, but not without somewhat more vigorous measures that those adoptable by a directorate of public health that has no time to do anything about the villagers except write a report that will – as it amply deserves – be filed away unread. The loss is calculable not only in human lives, but also in lowered production, in houses and property laid waste, not in taxes lost to the government, because for every person that dies, another can be found to work on the land, to pay the absentee or at least distant landlord his rent, supply enough surplus value for the revenue department.

Come back to the principle of curing by a small dose of the substance that kills-an idea that goes back to Hippocrates or even earlier. This can easily be overdone or misapplied. Potassium cyanide interrupts the heart rhythm in fantastically small doses, but so far as I know, it cannot be used to start again a heart that has stopped beating, reduce the dose, as you will. Koch, one of the greatest of bacteriologists and the most meticulous of experimenters tried to compete with Pasteur by using tuberculin [the poison of the germ of consumption, first discovered by Koch himself] in the treatment of tuberculosis. The effects were deadlier to the patient than to the microbes and the problem of killing the germs without killing the patient has not be solved even to this day for tuberculosis as well as for many other diseases. The principle is sound, but applications need study and experiment. Ehrlich, for example, cured syphilis, not by a vaccine or serum developed from the microbe that infects, but by careful study of the chemistry of an arsenic compound atoxyl. As you all know, it took a series of 606 experiments, not counting the preliminary work at all to get to salvarsan, and even then the chemists and biologists kept on in the hope of a better one, one which would not kill inexplicably or deteriorate into a poison instead of curing. The principle was later extended to the germ of sleeping sickness. Its latest triumph is seen in the sulphonamide and sulphathiazole type of compounds of which the soldiers who have returned from the war will tell you so much.

There is another branch of medicine that carries unintentionally the pseudo-Marxist attitude consistently all through its practice. I refer to homoeopathy. This science (founded by Hahnemann who died just a hundred years ago) maintains rigidly that in very small doses the drug producing a given set of symptoms must cure the disease having those symptoms. More strictly, the homoeopaths discard the disease theory altogether and "cure the patient, not the disease". Their standard dilution is the 30th *potency*, each potency being a hundredfold dilution of the previous one. So, *30* indicates a dilution of 10^{-60}, starting from the original amount of one grain. Now the smallest known material particle, the electron, has mass of order 10^{-26} grain, and there is no known way of distinguishing between electrons derived from one substance and those of another. To put it rather mildly, there is virtually no chance whatsoever of even a single molecule of the original substance entering the final dose of medicine. Moreover, no diluent, not even doubly distilled water is as pure as the 30th potency would require, so that such dilution can hardly have any meaning.

The scientific attitude, however, is not to scoff at homoeopathy, nor to deny the cures its enthusiasts report, nor to ascribe them all to faith. Faith should also work its share in any other system of medicine. One must perform the comparison between homoeopathy and any other system of medicine under controlled conditions giving both treatments to properly randomised groups of patients, with careful and impartial observers to note the result. The technique of such experiments is well developed; if anyone wishes to finance the experiment, I shall be able to tell him just how it is to be designed, and to analyse the results by modern statistical methods. No reports of miraculous cures will be as conclusive as the test I propose. On the other hand, Indian enthusists for homoeopathy tell me that the trial would not be fair because so much depends upon the powers of the homoeopath who administers the dose, upon his accuracy of diagnosis and treatment; this is admitting the superiority of the recognized medicine, which is a system that may be mastered by study without any special and mysterious powers.

It would be useless to deny the great influence that Hahnemann had on medicine, in reducing excessive drugging, in persuading the doctor to give the human body a sporting chance to recover without having to fight both disease and drug. The orthodox physicians of Hahnemann's day gave him little attention. As good Marxists, you should inquire into the cause of this. Why is it that so vital a profession as medicine still retains the mentality of the primitive medicine man and the witch doctor? Why is it that recognized doctors are still loosed upon the world without having performed a single experiment on a really scientific basis? Has this something to do with the fact that best doctors in capitalist society have necessarily to live as parasites upon the class in possession of wealth? Is homoeopathy popular in India because there aren't enough regular doctors to attend all who need treatment? Because these doctors and their European medicines are much too costly for the Indian patient? Because the Indian patient is of the lower classes, which means the vast majority – fears or hates the doctor with foreign mannerisms and finds homoeopathy closest to the medicine he still recognizes, the medicine of *Āyurveda* based on the theory of the humours and ancient observations grown to ritual? What can you say of a country where professors are to be found teaching the electron theory of matter for gospel truth in the classroom and then swearing by homoeopathy at home? What are the basic contradictions in our own society that give rise to these interesting and unfortunate phenomena?

Lecture 8

In earlier times, when the relations of man to his environment were not clearly understood, human activity necessarily was covered by an obscuring veil of ritual. The great changes that followed, therefore, were of religious type. You should not wonder at the decay of a mass taste for theology, nor conclude that people of those days had the ability to follow quite obscure and complicated arguments on fine points of doctrine. Men sacrificed their lives either because the lives were not worth living under contemporary circumstances or because the new doctrine promised better life for them as well as for the rest of humanity. To be able to fight for simple things like food, the right to the fruits of one's labour, the right to work and to rest, to live a healthy life, to receive proper accommodation and education – all this is a very recent achievement, a materialistic one; idealists fought for the highest ideals and the lowest fulfillments. The new religious system mould redress some grievance as an incidental by product, would crystallize out into a productive form not much superior to the old; the tide of human suffering had to flow on under another name. From a brief revolutionary upsurge at the beginning, every religious system settles down to preach in favour of the class in possession; it becomes an opiate for the people instead of a cure for their misery.

Buddhism in India has a social function to perform in its origins. The country (U. P. and Bihar) was torn by war between little princelings; all the older religion could say then was that the king who sacrificed more animals to the gods at a *yajnya* would gain the victory. The results were clear, a slaughter of farm animals, and a slaughter of human beings to follow. Buddhist *ahiṃsā* was on an immediately practical level, stopped the double slaughter, inculcated social virtues, created a class of teachers, the monks, who were clearly not actuated by the profit motive. The religion managed to provide necessary doctrinal support for what was a great need of the times, a strong centralized monarchy. We can barely glimpse the rise of a new type of merchant in the Gangetic plain, and the reorientation of trade towards new, hitherto unopened regions in the south. It is not an accident that Asoka is at once the first monarch of the whole of India, and the first Buddhist monarch. But with the settling down of the new forms of trade and of rule, the religion became cumbrous, its vast monasteries with their immense holdings uneconomic. It had to disappear except in places like Tibet where it became a form of the state, and where production was in any case comparatively undeveloped.

The most extraordinary of these religious quasi-revolutions may be studied in the rise and atrophy of Islam. In its original form it was effectively a new and democratic type of existence. It swept rapidly over the overtaxed provinces of the

Roman Empire, over the decayed remnants of Sassanian Persia, over a part of India as well. People would not fight against this new system in favour of an older one which sucked their blood. Often, they had nothing to fight with, being disarmed [as today] by their rulers in order to protect the class in exploitative possession. Islam could liberate social energy when it was an innovation; with a small measure of success, it tended to settle down into another stratified society much as does the dust in a house after all the rugs are given a good shaking up indoors. The only change was that a different set of people assumed the essential prerogatives of the class formerly in possession. The religious form remains in India, where its effects are most keenly felt. It is to the interest of the ruling power to emphasize its importance without emphasizing the cause of this importance: that the third of the population which professes this religion has about a tenth or less of the vital wealth. Even this wealth is of the older type, the semi-feudal landed property of the *nawab* and the *zamindar*, about as productive or unproductive as it has been throughout the ages. The banks, the factories, the major portion even of the ordinary trade of the country is in the hands of other Indians than the Muslims and it is precisely these modern forms of capital which are dangerous rivals to the power of that foreign capitalist class which runs the government of Britain and therefore of its empire. The class basis of communal riots, the economic background of religious tension will become obvious to anyone who compares the structure of Hindu-Muslim riots in Bombay with those of Rangoon where the land is [or was before the Japanese conquest] owned by Muslim capitalists, or of Mauritius where the labourers are Hindu with Muslims as the richer Indian settlers.[2]

2 DDK's annotation: The first aggressors belong to different communities in each case, with the administrative agents of foreign capital propping up the financially weaker.

Lecture 9

Dialectical materialism cannot predict the rise of any one great man, or even of some great man, at a given epoch. It can at best say why certain great men were effective, This gives a handle to those who fall back upon the "great man" theory of history, so dear to all fascists and in a way so neatly ingrained into the contemporary Indian mind. The *Führerprinzip* is not restricted to Germany. Those that worship it will find it difficult to explain why Mussolini and Kemal Atat¨urk, the senior and in most ways abler dictators fell behind in the race with Hitler who seems a lunatic by comparison. The reason is that in power politics what counts is the horsepower, the productive power of the nation, and not the brain power of the titular leader. The question in India is not whether the Mahatma is a better thinker than someone else who sets up as his rival, not which of the two could claim a better record as a lawyer, which of them professes doctrines that suit the economically better developed and expanding class? Under what circumstances, with what damming up of the normal channels of capitalist expansion, with what grave proximity of a revolution, what economic frustration, can a country like Germany follow the lead of a Hitler? Germany was perhaps the most civilized country in the world, certainly the most advanced in science, in 1913 when Hitler was a vagabond professing rudiments of much the same crazy ideas. What is the cause of the perversion?

In science and literature or art the great man might seem much harder to dispose of. Is it not a Newton who makes the science of his day? Can any Marxist predict the inevitability of a Dante? Let us make a small distinction at the start. Science is cumulative, like capitalist and machine production to which it is indeed most intimately related, science and the history of science are one, in that modern science can advance only by assuming the whole of the useful and relevant portion of its past. This is why Marxism applies to science. Even in a backward country like India, I can get a B. A. or a B. Sc. student or an undergraduate to solve problems that would certainly have baffled Newton, being well outside the mental horizon Newton had developed. But this achievement has become possible only by a mastery of the calculus that Newton initiated without developing it to the modern level, and without making much didactic use in his *Principia*. It is not equally true, however, that the great writer today needs master Shakespeare and Plato, no matter what the language and country in which he writes. Shakespeare does not imply the preexistence of Plato as Newton does of Euclid, Galileo, and Descartes. So also with the patriotic assertion that our great past is incomparable, seeing the great rsis and sages it produced, the great religious leaders that tortured themselves for the good of mankind. If you look into medieval European saints' lives, say that of Romuald, you will find actions that match in self-torturing asceticism and idiocy anything done in India. Sages of this type die, and leave little behind except a mysterious ununderstood doctrine. The next sage (if any) has to begin all over again from scratch to attain the mysterious powers, including that of levitation, digesting poisons, stopping his heartbeats, and so on. Note that I do not deny these powers; digesting nitric acid is certainly a well-authenticated yogic achievement today, as also control over heartbeats [considered not subject to voluntary action by most western physicians]; levitation I believe due to the misunderstanding of an ancient technical term, *uḍḍāyanam* that probably denotes hypnotism. But do these feats prove that the social and ethical doctrine the yogi professes is sound? Do they give any return to society for the pain in which his mother bore him, the food with which the tiller of the soil [ultimately] supplies him? Pasteur worked as hard as any rsi, suffered far greater pains in working, half paralyzed and incredibly neglected, with the most dangerous microbes and their poisons. His legacy was to all mankind, frees humanity from a great scourge, and the work can be understood by [and should be taught to] every high school boy, without specially mysterious powers. Research could begin where Pasteur left off, yogic attainment cannot.

Lecture 10

In many cases the great man acts as a catalyst. In chemistry many reactions cannot take place except in the presence of a substance that takes no direct part in the finished product, may be recovered intact after the reaction is complete. Spongy platinum is one such substance; the enzymes that promote your digestion (if you can get anything to digest) play the same role. Human society produces its own catalysts. This, if any, is the leadership principle. If there is human discontent, a great social need in a sufficiently large number of people, there must arise one or more men who will act as the spark to touch off an explosion. The police technique in India as in other countries is founded on this: keep the spark away and the powder cannot ignite; where you have freedom of speech or thought, it is a recognition by the classes in possession that there isn't powder enough for any serious explosion. So, Newton's science was necessary for developing the means of production of his day, in particular for the increasingly vigorous navigation of England; more accurate tables of the moon, hence a theory of lunar movement, of celestial mechanics, of mechanics in general with the inverse square law of gravitational attraction were required. Other people besides Newton were also on the right track, so that the discoveries would have been made sooner or later. On the other hand Newton wrote a great deal on theology, made what seemed to him profound researches on the length of the sacred cubit in the Bible – trash which is glossed over apologetically even by his most appreciative biographers.

One of the greatest men of all times both in the arts and in science was Leonardo la Vinci. What remains of his works is enough to convince anyone of the fact. He designed airplanes that might at least have been able to make small flights. There are sketches of tanks and improved weapons for warfare in his notebooks; his maps were superb, his pin-manufacturing machine seems to have been practicable and would have brought him a fortune if he could have made it; city planning really begins with him. Even his paintings show him to have been an experimenter. But the society of his day was not ready for him. Cesare Borgia found it better to attempt his conquest of Italy with poison and intrigue, to spend his money on jewels rather than on experimenting with Leonardo's military ideas. The court of Milan admired Leonardo's paintings and put him to work at designing shows with stage settings and costumes. The precious notebooks he left behind with an unworthy pupil were scattered piecemeal by that creature for a little paltry gain or to placate some rich noble who called for a specimen – we have to piece the torn remnants together very carefully today for a just appreciation of Leonardo's achievements.[3] But note again that every single one of these achievements were made by others in later times, just as the unpublished mathematical ideas in Gauss' notes were developed by others who never saw the notes themselves and had not Gauss' giant intellect. Leonardo had the misfortune to influence posterity only by his art, while Gauss had published a tremendous amount besides what he kept to himself, so that his influence on science and production is incomparably greater than that of Leonardo. The tradition of the East, including India, was as in Europe before the 17th century, always of secretiveness, of great ideas handed

3 DDK's annotation: Why can art be appreciated beyond the epoch of its production?

down untested and undeveloped from teacher to pupil, often degenerating into mere superstitious rigmarole in transition. The Europeans began publishing and communicating their ideas, the original learned societies dating from the 17th century and earlier, so that they had the advantage over us of cumulative social effort. This was necessary for and parallel to the capitalist development of their productive level, which made use of machine tools that represented accumulation of labour. They gained a great deal thereby while our pace was naturally much slower.

Lecture 11

Even in art and literature some periods seem to be favoured by nature or history, or the divine beings that are supposed to rule the fates of men. Bourgeois historians spend a lot of time and mental effort to no purpose discussing why the Periclean age in Athens, the Renaissance in Italy should be so important in the history of civilization. There is a double class basis to this sort of discussion: one deriving from the class prejudices of the historian as for example the attention given to Alexander's conquest of India [meaningless as he hardly penetrated into India proper] and its [purely imaginary] influence on Indian culture, quite a natural study for any British imperialistically bent historian. The second factor is almost always neglected, the class basis of the actual phenomenon itself. Look closer and you will find that the bloom of a new art form is the symptom of some great change in the productive relations of society, that it marks the emergence of some new class. The period of emergence is vital, just as force is not measured by the momentum but by the product of mass by *acceleration*. When the class develops to the stage where it can keep going by its momentum, there is a natural decay of art, of literature, of science, albeit with a certain lag in time. You may see the result of the British productive retreat not only upon British military science that led to Dunkirk, to Singapore, to Narvik in spite of years of heavy rearmament expenditure not only in unemployment and fantastic economic theories to justify it, not only in political reactionary theories – but also in literature and arts; you may rest assured that the position of British science relative to that of the rest of the world, as compared with its state at the turn of the century or the middle of the last, also shows decay. If you turn to H. A. L. Fisher's imposing "History of Europe", you will see that even lay appreciation of science has fallen abysmally low, the pontifical and totally reactionary historian discussing international currents of the last century gives first rank to Darwin and the theory of evolution, saying "Politics, too, were influenced by Darwinism". Unfortunately, the truth is just the opposite, Darwinism being a reflection of current free-trade politics of Great Britain which needed justification. The fossilized historian has no place for the influence of Faraday and Maxwell, of Gauss, Pasteur or the great German chemists of that century. Even the great men of history have to have their greatness measured by class standards of posterity.

The theory and the hero worship of great men is taking a very dangerous turn in India, with its nascent patriotism and powerful foreign rule. We have already produced one great mathematician, Srinivasa Ramanujan, and his name is bandied about with the utmost pride by people here who have not the energy nor the intelligence to master a single one of Ramanujan's papers. In fact, the history is tragic. Ramanujan's intellect was stifled by the treatment he received here, and he died at the age of thirty-five, of tuberculosis brought on by overwork and by malnutrition in his formative years. The best job he could get was that of a clerk in the Madras Port Trust. The mathematical training he received was given in England, where there was one mathematician, G. H. Hardy, intelligent enough to recognize merit; no one in India could claim half as much! Even the mathematics of Ramanujan was based on foreign discoveries, not on the Indian school which came to an end with Bhaskaracarya eight hundred years ago. The effect of Ramanujan's work was felt and manifested in the further researches of British workers, but nowhere in India because it is much easier to worship a hero than to study his work. Another great man, Tagore, has an unquestioned fame, but also no successor in Indian literature. The expanding class in Tagore's formative period was the class that had been ruined by the inroads of British trade, and had then been able to expand again by taking to new jobs and professions created by British administrative needs. This has now degenerated to a reactionary bureaucracy, its educational institutions to the wastebasket of all the professions. Tagore cannot even be read under such circumstances, let alone excelled.[4]

The most dangerous of effects deriving from the leadership principle come from the natural displacement that identifies great men with the men in power. This builds up in India a pyramid of incompetence from the highest government bureaucrat down to the last sedimentary bootlicker. These great men of the descending scale claim a privileged status that they derive from the glory of all great men, it is society that is obliged to them, not they to society. The extreme consequences of this theory were to be seen in the film that you must all have attended which made the French revolution an unfortunate and inexplicable personal accident which happened to Marie Antoinette. Our miniature great men forget that the most competent technician, doctor, engineer, scien-

---

4 DDK's annotation: He will be regarded as the last great man of his brief period, not the first of a new one, unless socialism comes to India with a …[?]. Note on the margin: Class basis of contemporary Indian scientists.

tist had to be maintained at the expense of society as a whole [though he may think that his father's wealth or a scholarship gained by his own early brilliance from a benign government supported him] till he himself became productive. The special qualification is a product of social labour, due to an appropriation of surplus value deriving from the labour of others; it cannot with justice be made the basis for a parasitic existence thereafter. With us, the less the competence, the greater the pretensions, the greater the claim upon society and its products.

Socialism as distinct from communism is the form of society that would insist upon equal opportunity for all, with equal pay for equal work. Even the Soviet Union has not reached this stage, though the worst inequalities have been redressed. That is because the problem of production has to be solved in the Soviet Union in the face of a continuous struggle against a deadly hostile environment. If production is below the threshold value, equality means equality of poverty, misery, helplessness. So inequality has often been created quite deliberately by the Soviet administration, not as a reward for political support or as distribution of patronage, but a stimulus to merit, an incentive to the solution of new problems that arise with its increasing tempo of production. It is a transient phase; even then, no one need starve or go without medical attendance; no man can start a bank or a factory, or build a house for rent with his money no matter how high his salary and how much he saves. The essential step at that level was socialization and planned use of the means of production. That has been achieved against all opposition.

Lecture 12

Materialism, you will hear many people say, is all right within its limits, but cannot be allowed to enter into the higher sphere of human life, the spiritual side of man should not be neglected. Life itself is inexplicable and not a manifestation of matter. This I deny flatly in its entirety. If we have yet or to understand many thing about life, we have as many or more to understand about matter. Most recent of developments have shown that there are chemicals, like the tobacco mosaic virus, that remain inert, "dead" substances as long as they are left in a bottle, but which begin to increase and multiply in much the same way as live bacteria if allowed to develop in a suitable medium. The work of Bergmann and his school makes it likely, even in our present state of knowledge that the active portion of the cells that make up our bodies, make up all animal bodies, and are called chromosomes perform the essential portion of their function merely by being proteinases with a definite chain molecule structure. Models can theoretically be built up out of nucleic acid platelet chains and the like which would have many of the properties associated with genes, and these genes carry most of what we all hereditary effects which are, be it understood, only expressible in terms of reaction to environment. The proteinase compounds would have the property of acting like the enzymes as catalysts, and at the same time of duplicating themselves. Life, to put the classic words of Engels in modern terminology, is the mode of existence of proteins.

There is no need for creation, none for a guiding spirit for evolution. As the earth cooled down from a molten sphere, the condensing vapours and enormous heat enabled many chemical compounds to be formed by mere chance meeting of the molecules under ordinary laws of chemistry. Among them some had the proteinase structure which enabled them to develop at the expense of the others that had not that structure but could serve as "food". The root developments must have been confined to small portions at first, because we know that many chemicals can exist in two mirror-image types of crystals, the dextro and the laevo-rotatory, in nature, they mostly exist in the laevorotatory shape, life being associated as a rule with left hand rotation of polarised light by the crystalline product in solution. These developing and self-reproducing chemicals could not go by themselves beyond a rather small limit till they had developed a protective surface membrane and formed the cell unit. The change of quality had necessarily to follow with change of quantity. Then nourishment could be absorbed by osmosis, the cell could split into two as soon as it grew beyond a certain size, the nucleus duplicating itself before the split. This was necessary because nourishment has to be absorbed through the surface which grows as the square of the linear dimension, but the total substance to be kept up grows much more rapidly, as the cube. Then comes a further step, certain cell divisions not splitting up. These cell groups had the advantage of size over monocellular organisms, could proliferate more rapidly, but had to develop separate functions and a more complex organization. During the course of development, these increasingly complex organisms had also to develop a larger inner contradiction, death sometimes associated with disease, or parasitism by simpler organisms or pieces of simpler organisms. So we go up the road of life, unpredictable in individual steps and yet consistent in the bulk, like all statistical effects. Changes in the evolutionary process could be caused by simple chance, such as that which governs the action of cosmic rays; we still see a part at least of this mechanism today as mutations. But mutations are in general lethal, kill their organism or lower its fitness to profit by the environment. In exceptional cases, a mutation increases the fitness, the survival value, the rate of breeding as against the rate of death, leading to an evolutionary advance. For survival is also a phenomenon of the aggregate, not of one individual.

Lecture 13

Human beings can change their environment much more than do other organisms, so that they can develop far more in extent. The grain we eat, rice, wheat, and such cereals actually are as artificial a product as the houses we live in. If all human activity ceased today, our houses and monuments would last for centuries, but the cereals would disappear except for unrecognizable wild forms within a single human generation. Similarly for fruit trees, and for most of the agricultural animals we use. Agriculture is not a natural phenomenon, it is a social activity. By taking to such activity man changed himself: as well as the grain on which he fed and which he had to develop from grasses by selection. Before that, he lived by feeding the cattle on grass, eating the grass seeds only in times of great famine; even pasturing cattle was a great step in advance of the period when the hunter followed migratory herds much as did the wolf. The wolf pack could not take the step of herding the wild cattle according to its convenience, of driving them with the season to better pasturage, of conserving their numbers: Therefore, the simple interaction of the wolf and the herd exercises no civilizing influence on either.

The selection of grass seeds showed that some were more productive when planted and cultured. Differences between various kinds of soil were then to be observed with respect to fertility of grain. The number of people who could live on a given amount of soil by hunting was much less than that which could survive by pasturage, and that in turn was far exceeded by those who cultivated grain. The evolutionary process, by increasing quantity, necessarily changed the social quality of the human beings and their groups. Evolution is the continual succession of the more efficient to the less; it is purely a material process, not an act of divine will. This holds for both biological and social evolution.

One of the factors now retarding evolution in human society is the invention of the society itself that interprets its concealed relationships within itself as well as with nature in terms of quite extraneous factors. Religion, reactionary as it becomes when fully developed, must also have had its day as a great civilizing influence. We can see that effect of Christianity in the middle ages, as we saw briefly the effect of Buddhism in India. The old Roman formula for capital punishment *sacer esto* [let him be sacrificed to the gods] represents an adjustment of later social needs to old and blind religious ritual; the condemned law-breaker is to be used to placate the ununderstood forces of nature, sacrificed to the gods to promote fertility of the land or whatever else may be thought necessary. Here, then, society begins to develop under the cover of and almost within the grooves formed by religious thought. Later on, the religion may become, as in the Roman empire, a purely formal affair with ritual intimately connected with the administrative apparatus, but not yet an opium of the people, not a promise of compensations in the next life for class-made misery in this one, not openly a spiritual apparatus for reducing the burden on the police force. In India, you can trace this development with the beginning of the caste system, in spite of our very scanty records, and follow its varying types down the ages. Then you will see that it is no accident that our Brahmins were the first to rush in such large numbers into the service of a foreign and very low caste government. Beefeating to an orthodox Hindu should theoreti-cally be far more heinous as a crime than cannibalism in Europe, but serving beefeating masters has not seemed impossible to our highest castes. Naturally, the same people deny most vigorously that there is anything to materialism and to class interest; it is the deep inner spiritual need of man that, according to them, has always been recognized in India as first. Their actions go beyond dialectic contradiction into mere logical contradictions, paradoxes, unless we explain them by pure self-interest of the class as a whole.

Lecture 14

I noted at the beginning the perversion that made the idealist out to be a good and noble man, the materialist to be a brute who tries solely for his own gain. The principal reason for this today is that our kind of materialism questions the necessity and justice of capitalist social structure. It is much nicer for those now in possession to exclude such disturbing logic by maligning it, though they go further than mere slander in their use of repressive methods. There is, however, one point to be considered in the argument, because some students of materialism fail to reason their way that far. Is there any such thing as good and evil for the materialist? What is absolute truth, if any such exists? What is freedom? Or are these all-meaningless terms invented by an insidious bourgeoisie to fuddle the proletariat? Are they all empty of content on the grounds that one can do what one likes because after all one's actions are conditioned by environment, by the form of society?

Freedom is the recognition of necessity. It is not intrinsically and absolutely necessary that poor people should starve in the midst of plenty unless they are denied access to the fruits of human labour, or even to simple means of livelihood. But the starvation, unemployment, maldistribution are necessities in the capitalistic productive system, which needs a profit motive to get owners to sanction production, and a constant pool of the unemployed to keep wages down to the lower threshold value. The necessity of starvation is, therefore, not meaningless but an integral portion of a given social structure. To remove this particular necessity forever it is necessary and sufficient to change the social structure, not to a more primitive but to a more advanced form. The very process of discovering the root cause takes you one step towards its negation.

This is a main principle of science as well as of Marxism. The scientist cannot define cause and effect with the rigour that the abstract philosophers might demand, but he does well enough to make things work better than they did before his discoveries. Observation can often be only indirect, can take place only by reasoning from the effect that is evident when one changes a given situation, when one negates it. There can, naturally, be no observation that does not change the observed to some extent, because in the final analysis observation is only possible because of the interactions of matter. To take two examples: Many people were blind in former ages, and had to pray for sight or resign themselves to the blind necessity for blindness. Progress came when the necessity was analysed, and the eye studied as an optical instrument, as a physiological organ. Then it was found that certain forms of blindness could be cured by glasses, and we merely call these shortsightedness, or farsightedness. Study of the eye by itself would not have negated the necessity without the equivalent of a lens-grinding technological accomplishment; but if you can go deeper into the matter, you will see that study of the eye as an optical instrument, theory of optics and refraction, of light lens-grinding all go hand in hand, develop together. The most idealistic of sages couldn't sit down under a greenwood tree to meditate the whole matter out by the mysterious powers of his own mind.

The second example is from bacteriology, when some workers discovered that some cultures of bacteria, particularly of those that cause intestinal disturbances and disease [like typhoid, cholera, some forms of dysentery] tended to clear up without any cause. The bacilli just disappeared. This was observed also by Hankin of cholera bacteria in the waters of the Jumna. D'Herelle found that a drop from such a cleared solution put into a fresh culture of the same bacilli cleared up the entire second lot in even less time. A drop transferred to a third culture showed even greater power, and so on through successive passages. This looks as if we were to revive the mysterious powers of our sacred rivers, and to arrive at the principle of homoeopathy ridiculed a few sections ago. But systematic experiment showed the cause here. The bacteria are broken up by a disease of their own, perhaps a small portion of the bacterium which frees itself and can feed on the whole organism like a disease of the organism, This agent, though it could not be seen, is living, can be killed by heat and by chemicals, can be measured in size (and perhaps even made visible by our new electron microscopes). The experiments of d' Herelle and the other scientists that joined him cleared off earlier misconceptions. There is bacteriophage in the sacred rivers, as I had verified from the samples I took in the Ganges. Only this is not due to any puranic sanctity, but to the sewage that flows into the river, and the unburnt corpses that are thrown into it. Our ancient rsis did not worship the river from some mysterious knowledge of its properties, nor is cowdung prescribed by ancient Hindu ritual in so many devastatingly nauseous ways because of its undeniable bacteriophagic content; the cowdung like the waters of the Ganges contains much that is noxious, and human dung contains more bacteriophage!

We can reach a working definition of goodness. Whatever increases human welfare is good, whatever hampers humanity in its endeavour is bad. When a child cries for hunger, as happens so often in this country, it is good to plan a world where such things will not happen. But it is good also to feed it at once if food is available; it seems to me less desirable to quiet the child as is done most often by the indigent mother worker, by dosing it with a little opium. It seems to me downright evil to discourse learnedly in a well-fed manner to quite distant city audiences of the very best people that India must remain backwards because its mothers don't know any better than to quiet children with harmful drugs [a monopoly of the paternal government] rather than to feed them with food that they do not possess.

In all these matters there is the statistical element. We make abstractions when we isolate some quality and these have to be made upon a statistical basis. One man may claim quite sincerely that starvation is good for the child; some children might be overfed, some might not like to eat some meals. The truth in these matters is what remains on the balance, after opposing individual wishes have cancelled out. As a rule these wishes themselves have been conditioned by the environment in which the individual has been reared. It is, therefore, possible at critical moments to mislead even great movements, though not forever. In places like Germany and England, where labour had made great advances, it was possible after World War I to lead the entire movement away from communism or socialism. In talking with American workmen before 1929, it was obvious that their chief reaction to socialistic doctrine lay in great fear of losing what they had – which was more than the labour of any other country, and even more than the bourgeoisie of many backward colonial and semicolonial lands. The response to John Lewis and the CIO after the great depression shows that their eyes had been opened to the fundamental insecurity of their position, and if they insist in not going all the way, there are more wars in store for them, irrefutable arguments for communism. It would be better if they could reason out for themselves the superiority of a socialistic form of production which enables a far less developed country like the Soviet Union to hold out against and finally crush Hitler's wonderful machine.

Chapter 2

On Statistics

Modern statistics, as contrasted with descriptive statistics of the older type, differs primarily in being a guide to action, which implies more accurate results with an estimate of the error and greater rapidity of working with smaller samples observed. It is not realised that ancient statistics was also in its own way a guide to action, its lack of credit today being due solely to its clumsier apparatus and, with more reason, to the distressing quality of its findings from the point of view of a certain class of people.

The standard types of descriptive statistics are the ancient Roman census which was after all a stock taking for the purposes of the State; its logical continuation in feudal times is the Domesday book of William the Conqueror which (allowing for the changed circumstances) is much the same thing, namely a bit of stocktaking for taxation purposes.

I might illustrate the rise of a new class and a new way of thinking by pointing out to you the change in European literature in the 17th and the 18th centuries. The older literature dealt with persons of heroic stature who specialize in humanly impossible knightly adventures. The tradition begins with the *Chanson de Roland*, to continue through the entire Arthurian Round Table cycle and the deeds of the Paladins of Charlemagne. On the other hand, when you look down into later literary efforts, you find quite unheroic average figures as for example Lesage's *Gil Blas* or Marivaux's *Paysan parvenu* or the most attractive of them all, Voltaire's *Candide* who passes through adventures which are quite romantic in themselves but in which his behaviour is such that the reader can say "this might happen to anyone". It is not realised, however, that this change in literature corresponds to an appreciation of the fact that human being have a certain average, a certain standard or norm, which in itself is well worth studying. The terms "average man" had to wait until well into the 19th century but the concept definitely existed long before Voltaire whose charming story on the subject is entitled "*L'homme a quarante écus*" deals with a person who has forty minted pieces of money, which was the average wealth of a Frenchman at that time. The point is that someone had made a fairly reliable estimate of the total national wealth and of the total population, thereby reaching the estimate of average wealth and actually showing the possibility of a statistical approach to the whole subject. That is, the 'average men' who figure in the literature of the 19th century depend upon a statistical attitude towards humanity. This naturally is to be expected from the long tradition of study which lies back of Sully, Bodin, Turgot and the entire school of physiocrats; it also implies the rise of a new type of people who liked to think in this manner peculiar to the French bourgeoisie.

Let us look now at the development of the need for a wider kind of statistics than that necessary only for budget and taxation. In the year 1542, for example, we find that at Antwerp wagers are being laid against the sex of on unborn child. A merchant would undertake to pay 30 livres if the offspring were a girl whereas in gratitude he would receive from the mother 48 livres if a son were born. Or there may be a wager that the exchange rate would be at a 2% premium or discount; there would be other wagers which would deal with the failure or success of a certain standing crop or the safe home-coming of a given ship. These look like gambles but you will see at once that these are a primitive type of insurance. The thirty livres go towards the girl's dowry, whereas the son could earn his keep and the 48 livres besides. Insurance of cargoes goes right back to Roman and Grecian times. Nevertheless, with statistics undeveloped, and a very poor control of the subject as well as very few cases coning up, the merchant who undertook this enterprise was virtually a gambler. Briefly, if you insure one man for 7 million rupees you are running a far greater risk than if you insure 7 thousand men for 1000 rupees each, The fuller development comes in the year 1836, when the Belgian A. Quetelet published his book on Social Physics. Quetelet, to who the term "average man" is due, was the first person to break down any modern census figures. He found among other things that crime depended to a regularly predictable extent upon the economic level of the class under consideration. The poorer the class the greater incidence of crime, independently of the locality. It was also found that mortality depended with a tremendous regularity upon professions. If a man has to work for his living in a military profession in a period of constant warfare he certainly risks his life in an open manner. But it was not realised that forcing a certain worker to work with lead – as for example types of glazing – or phosphorus and sulphur as in match-making, or mercury as for felt hats, amounted to sentencing that worker to die a few years earlier, or in the last case to lunacy as well. I should like to point out that this discovery of Quetelet led in the long run to the discrediting of statistics as a science whereas Quetelet himself believed that he had discovered new scientific laws whose inexorable character really frightened him. What he had discovered were not laws of nature but actually laws of a certain particular type of industrial society.

Such discoveries are used nowadays in building up the basis of such a gigantic financial development as the insurance business, those importance I need not explain to anyone in Bombay who can walk down a single mile of Hornby Road and read the signboards around him. Mortality tables were first made privately by the actuaries themselves in a very crude fashion and from the late 17th century onwards are available from census figures. The differences of mortality in different occupations are fully recognized and allowed for in the premium charged by the insurance company. But insurance is no longer speculation or gamble for the simple reason that the data from millions of policies is available, and that millions of people get themselves insured so that the statistical average can apply very well. In fact the data from insurance companies has allowed tremendous advances to be made in the science of demography, so that we can predict years in advance the approximate amount of the population as well as its structure by age groups. In the U.S.A. for example manufacturers pay a great deal of attention to this. It was known before the war that the number of children born was decreasing due to falling birth rate and the predictions based on this warned manufacturers of school text books and children's clothes to allow for so many million articles less annually. Such forecasts are not only possible but absolutely essential in a country where mass production is the rule. In other words, this type of statistics is also a guide to action, *provided it pays the right people to act upon it.* On the other hand if it be discovered that conditions led to the shortage of certain commodities, the action generally taken is that of attempting to secure a corner in those commodities, regardless of its effect on the lives of the consumers; this happened, for example, in the Bengal famine. It is difficult to commend such action upon any basis, statistical or otherwise. I take just one more example, that of Lotka's findings from the data accumulated by the Metropolitan Life Insurance Company of New York. Among other things he showed that the general USA death rate was decreasing slowly, but with absolute regularity, up to the year 1918 when a sudden rise occurred because of the epidemic of Spanish influenza. But after that epidemic was over, the death rate fell again succeeding years not to the straight line on which it had been declining but another straight line decidedly lower than but parallel to the first. The conclusion was that the Spanish influenza had killed those with the least powers of resistance whether physical or financial and those that survived were under the circumstances of contemporary society, fitter to live. Possibly some genius may arise here to prove a similar beneficial action for the Bengal famine.

People were not willing to face up to the idea that the structure of society might itself force certain classes to criminality, which was really a result marked out in Quetelet's work. Towards the end of the last century eminent Italian criminologists following a great tradition founded by the jurist Cesare Beccaria began to investigate the criminal's circumstances. Among them Lambroso, Ferraro, and Mantegazza studied the physique of convicted criminals only to discover that there was a criminal type. Criminals had abnormalities of vision, asymmetric skulls and various types of impediments. Ergo there was a criminal type, the criminal could not help himself, his nature was crooked because his head was crooked. This kind of research (which would not be taken as accurate by current standards) attracted a great deal of attention because it drew emphasis away from the economic question. No one asked why the man's head had become deformed, whether poverty in childhood had anything to do with it, nor even whether the confusion of cause and effect might not have existed in such researches. Later on, these same scientists undertook to examine in the same way men of superior intellect, supposedly valuable members of society such as artists, musicians and even professors of mathematics. Being honest men they had to publish their findings which were, alas, that the heads of these geniuses were also not symmetrical and they too suffered from a considerable number of impediments. Nevertheless society chose not to pay any attention to this, preferring to drop the entire subject in a quiet but discreet fashion.

At this stage statistics becomes the joke that it is often mistaken to be. No statistician today can deliver a popular lecture without quoting that British statesman who gave vent to a classical utterance "Gentlemen – There are three kinds of lies; lies, damned lies, and statistics". The idea is that one can prove anything he likes by reference to the appropriate set of statistics. I once made a collection of jokes of this sort about statistics of which one or two may be given here. At a medical conference an eminent child specialist gave the conclusion of 15 years of painstaking research to prove that the first day of life was the most dangerous as having the highest recorded average mortality of 28.2%. His rival jumped up with the remark that this research was all bosh and that the last day of life was much more dangerous because then the mortality was 100%. In another case two very learned people were having an intellectual tea with an even more intellectual conversation which ran somewhat as follows: "My dear colleague – I find that the latest statistics show men graduates of our colleges as having

1.4 children each whereas the lady graduates have 3.7 children each. What does this prove? The answer came immediately, "Obviously this shows that women have more children than men." One could go on like this for ever but I only want to make it clear to you that statistics had fallen into considerable disrepute.

From this stage it had to be rescued by the need for application to branches of science in which experiment could not be refined beyond a certain level. In physics of the classical type one can measure more accurately, or make pure alloys or refine the experiment almost indefinitely. In modern physics on the contrary, electrons, cosmic rays and such new discoveries behave in a highly individualistic manner. In fact they behave like biological specimens, that is to say the output of a certain type of grain planted in a field or the blood content of a given strain of mice, or fish in a certain lake. In this case you can only observe but not refine the observation. Nevertheless some method is needed for drawing accurate conclusions. That is to say a guide for immediate action. It was a biological science that developed statistics itself as a basic and even a fundamental science. The first stop in the modern direction came in the year 1908 from the mind of an able mathematician employed by the great breweries of Messrs. Guinness. They had to find from experiment in small plots which variety of barley would give the greatest yield and what types of fertilizers would increase this yield most economically. Now it is impossible to count every grain of barley and experimenting with all their land year after year for different varieties world not only be very costly but would also not give valid result for the simple reason that rainfall conditions also differ from year to year. Finally the ground is not uniform so that soil variation has also to be taken into account along with the possible action of insects, weeds and other causes that might affect the grain. Nevertheless the method was worked out and can give good results using not more than a couple of dozen plots each the size of a small room provided the plots are selected in certain random unbiased fashion. The methods were later worked up with far more detail, accuracy, penetration, and insight by R. A. Fisher who is today the great name in modern statistics. These methods are now applicable not only to biology and to cosmic rays but to sociology, archaeology and even financial questions. Statistics may now be regarded as a science rather than as a joke or a laborious but painful method of description. With a small sample, often less than 5% of the whole, we can draw conclusions about the entire aggregate and in addition say what the error of our estimate happens to be. This point has not always been grasped by statisticians of the older school, primarily economists, who use new methods mechanically without realizing that statistics even of the most improved type cannot be a substitute for intelligence. For example, I recall an economic survey of Poona City undertaken in the years 1937–38 which chose one house out of every fifteen for its sample without attention to appropriate randomisation and without testing for bias. The conclusions were published only in the year 1945 by which time the findings had been completely invalidated by the pressure of war, by the influx of military and other new Government establishments and by the construction of tremendous new factories for which the working population was based upon Poona. The only excuse for the sampling survey of this sort is its rapidity as well as accuracy and its estimate of error; all three were absent in the case cited.

Let me give you a concrete example of what a precise scientific prediction is like and then show you that such a prediction can be made also by using statistical methods. Just a hundred years ago the Newtonian theory of gravitation had began to be suspected because the outermost planet then known, namely Uranus, did not follow the path predicted for it by Newton's laws. Uranus had been discovered by Herschel (then a professional musician) an amateur astronomer who prepared his own lenses and telescopes. The question now was as to whether the Newtonian theory with its inverse square law of gravitation had to be modified or whether there existed another planet whose pull could account for the discrepancies between theory and observation as regards the movement of Uranus through the sky. Two unknown but ambitious young men independently undertook this task of explaining the discrepancy on the hypothesis of an unknown planet. Of these Adams had the misfortune to send his conclusions to the Astronomer Royal who quietly filed them away, the other Urbain Jean-Jacques Leverrier wrote to the astronomer at Berlin Dr. Galle to the effect that if Dr. Galle would point his telescope to a part of the sky where he had recently chartered his stars he would find within the field of that telescope a new heavenly body, a star that moved, in fact a planet, and on the 23rd September 1846 Galle had the stirring experience given to so few of finding a new planet swim into his ken. As Arago put it to the French Academy of Sciences in reporting on the great discovery of the young French astronomer, M. Leverrier had not to see his planet with a telescope; he saw it at the end of his pen. This is the classical example of a prediction in science which was spectacular as well as fully confirmed by experiment. I could give you many such in pure science where statistics was the tool of analysis but these will not be as spectacular as the one that I shall now call to your attention. In the U.S.A. a journal called the *Literary Digest* had started the custom of taking straw votes among, its readers by asking them to fill out certain types of coupons on various questions of interest and this had led them to a quite successful study of prediction in events such as elections. In 1936 they announced their intention of taking another poll of this sort for the forthcoming presidential election. The editor was annoyed to read the assertion from a young public opinion expert, Dr. Gallup, that the *Literary Digest* would show a vote of 56% against Roosevelt and 44% for him, while the real facts would show an overwhelming majority of votes cast for Roosevelt, and a still larger percentage of votes in the electoral college under the peculiar American system of presidential elections. What annoyed the Literary Digest most was that this assertion was made six weeks before their survey actually started. Yet when they had finished counting well over two million of their returns they did announce the conclusion that Gallup had said they would announce while the election results again proved Gallup's own forecast completely while driving the *Literary Digest* to ruin. All that Gallup had done was to follow the method laid down by Fisher. He had counted, with trained observers, a small percentage of the total population of the U.S.A. in which were represented all groups in every locality according to their appropriate strength. That is, in the sample Dr. Gallup chose at random, he made certain that working class voters, voters of the professional class like doctors and lawyers, religious groups such as Protestants of various denominations, Roman Catholics, Jews and racial minorities were all properly represented and picked at random from local directories without personal knowledge. Predictions of this sort enable us to say that statistics has a claim to be more than a joke, in fact to be a very respectable science.

In modern statistics the estimate of the error is a specially important point, for our statistics no longer deals only with averages and percentages but also with the amount of variation. An important function of statistics is that of 'costing' or giving the amount of information in a certain sample which in effect is equivalent to showing how sharply the mechanism of observation can focus upon a given problem. The statistician, if consulted *before* the observations are taken and supplied with some minimum data about the nature of the population can say how best to allocate the energy available for observation, or to what degree of accuracy information may be obtained from a given amount of available resources, The results have to be expressed in terms of probability which has misled many people. When we say that a certain result is significant in that there is only a chance in 20 or one in a hundred of being exceeded, we are not speaking in terms of the race course but are actually using the same kind of reasoning that you use, almost instinctively, but actually because of long experience, when you allow for a given amount of time to catch a bus or a train or for a certain letter to reach a certain correspondent. Naturally the allowance made depends not only upon your previous experience of such happenings but also upon the importance you may happen to attach to the outcome of the particular event, whether it is a matter of routine or a matter of importance to which a cash value can be attached, or a matter of life and death. What has not been grasped is that in all cases of this sort where noticeable variation necessarily occurs – and this means in all cases where scientific observation has to be repeated – one can never get an infallible answer but only an answer that is likely to be right in almost all cases. Statistics tries to give you a definite estimate to how often you are likely to be right *in the long run*.

Nevertheless, the fact still remains that very few people are interested in statistics itself as a pure science and those people have no voice in the affairs of the world. We still have the habit of taking conclusions that are pleasing to us and ignoring the rest. For example Gallup was able to say that the vast majority of the people who voted for Roosevelt did not approve of Roosevelt's ideas about the Supreme Court reform in spite of which Roosevelt took his third term election an a mandate for driving the Supreme Court to acquiescence. If it comes to that Gallup does not make his living by forecasting elections but by predicting the popularity of a certain commercial product say a new soap or a new brand of coffee or a particular kind of advertising programme for the business people of the USA. He is, inevitably, subservient to the interests of the business community and his election forecasts are more a sort of advertising for the superior accuracy of the methods he uses. In the matter of these public opinion surveys, I might point out in them two types of results, qualitative and quantitative. Gallup's are quantitative, and for this, a precise, accurate statistical mechanism is indispensible. But others, as for example the great anthropologist B. Malinowski used a totally different approach to reach qualitative results. Malinowski had made quite remarkably acute observations on living conditions upon the Trobriana islanders using his own western education as a background against which to measure the mentality of the primitive people being studied. Then he turned this method as well the background he himself acquired by his studies over to observing the British public, his inquiries were directed towards asking all kinds of people through the medium of trained impartial observers as to why they did or did not do certain things and noting down the results verbatim. This showed for example that the football pool which is virtually a swindle in Great Britain is nevertheless popular only because it is the sole method by which a member of the British working class has any chance of clearing enough money to rise out of that class. He investigated questions as to why pubs (places where alcoholic drinks are served) are so popular and what time of the day or week they were specially popular, why people do not vote in spite of the franchise, and so on. The method still continues in Great Britain under the name of Mass Observation, but its findings have raised the expected opposition and antipathy and the mass observers are often regarded as gratuitous snoopers in spite of the fact that the Ministry of Information found it very useful to avail itself of their service on questions such as that of morale and rationing which are after all qualitative rather then quantitative questions. In India we could use this type of qualitative analysis to find for example not how many Muslims wanted Pakistan (which would need a sampling survey) but what kind of Pakistan was meant by what particular type or types of Muslims. I might add that the question cannot be settled in any other way except such observations, for the electorate is not a random survey sample of the total Muslim population and victory at the polls says virtually nothing about the actual desire of the masses about which every politician can speak interminably. The great example of such observation is of course the work of the supreme realist of our times, Vladimir Illyich Ulianov, better known as Lenin. He kept his pulse so accurately not only on the voiced but even on the unspoken desire of the masses that he was able to guide an entire Revolution in its most critical period and through most unfavourable circumstances to a successful consummation. With him we reach the stage not only of observing society but changing it. But if I go any further into his achievements, I shall be preaching Bolshevism in the sacred precincts of Bombay House and so must stop here.

CHAPTER 3

Atomic Energy for India

The word energy is associated in the minds of most of you with steam engines, electric supply, diesel or petrol motors, water-turbines and perhaps windmills. The word evokes others like horsepower, kilowatts, and calories; perhaps also electricity and petrol bills, price per ton of coal, and increased taxes for the Five-year Plans. I want only to point out to you that these technical, social and economic considerations go very deep, down to the foundations of human society. With the coming of atomic energy they have reached a stage which is critical for the whole of mankind, far above mere personal considerations.

We rarely think of the simplest and most familiar type of energy, namely that derived from food – though far too many in this world still have to think of food as the one overwhelming need for their lives. Man needs from 2000 to 4000 calories of nutritional energy per day, according to the climate, conditions of work, and type of food taken. In our ordinary discussions of a balanced diet, vitamins etc. this elementary fact is often forgotten; namely that the value of food depends upon the amount of energy it can release in the human or animal body. To make this energy available in the digestive system, man needs to have his food cooked by fire, which means another form of energy obtained by burning fuel. The history of mankind begins with the first steps above the animal stage, when man learned to control fire, and began to produce food instead of just gathering it.

The next step, the formation of human society proper, with division of labour and differentiation of social functions, was made possible only by more power: that of animals such as cattle or horses for agriculture and transport. Human labour-power was also used in greater quantity, whether slave labour or that of paid drudges. Other sources such as windmills and water wheels helped. The industrial revolution could not have been realised before the discovery and the extensive use of the steam engine in the early 19th century. Man succeeded in the conversion of fire-energy into mechanical work. Electricity lay in the transmission of energy to places distant from the point of generation. The steam engine used directly meant chains, driving rods, gears, cables, or some such mechanical transmission. You know how much human society has been changed by electricity in a single lifetime, say the lifetime of Edison.

What is the ultimate source of all such power? Food-grains, fruit, nuts etc. store their energy from sunlight, which is absorbed by the living plant, along with carbon dioxide from the atmosphere, water vapour and other substances. Cellulose thus made is also the main source of the energy stored in firewood. Coal and oil are simply organic matter converted by deep burial in the earth for millions of years. Hence, all these forms of energy come from the sun, the difference being in the method by which the energy is stored. The chemical processes involved may be described as molecular change. The breakdown of the energy in food and fuel is also chemical and molecular. The molecules may change, their atoms do not. For wind-power, the sun heats up some of the air, which rises, and is replaced by other, cooler air. These air-currents drive the windmill. Water-power is similarly drawn from the sun without chemical change. The water evaporated by the sun's heat rises, forms clouds, and comes down again as rain. What we utilise is the flow of rainwater from a higher to a lower level.

The electric energy, which appears on our monthly bills (in the few Indian homes fortunate enough to have the supply) is measured in kilowatt-hours. One-kilowatt hour is equivalent to one horsepower for about an hour and twenty minutes. It is also equivalent to a little more than 860,000 calories of heat. But these are the equivalents when nothing is lost in the change from one form to the other. In practice, something is always lost. No transformation of energy is a hundred percent efficient, and most of them are decidedly inefficient. The machine loses a good deal of energy in friction; electricity is lost in transmission, and by leakage; heat is radiated away. These losses are physically inevitable, and a fundamental property of matter. But energy is also a fundamental property of matter, apart from the chemical changes and mechanical processes. Matter cannot be destroyed by ordinary mechanical or chemical processes. But if it could be annihilated in some way, an equivalent amount of energy must appear. This was finally proved by Einstein, who summed it up in the formula $E = mc^2$ which gives the absolute energy available from a given amount of matter.

Atomic energy is fundamentally different from molecular energy. For the first time in history, man has been able to duplicate the solar processes for himself on earth. Solar energy depends upon the breakdown of the atomic nucleus, with the resultant emission of heat, X-ray radiation, longer [wavelength electromagnetic] waves, and particles such as electrons, neutrons and the like. These last correspond to the smoke and ashes of ordinary fuel, but are much more dangerous to man. The electricity cannot be utilised directly.

The main useful output of atomic nuclear reactions is still the heat, which has then to be converted into power like any other source of heat. This might seem wasteful, but is much less wasteful than other forms of conversion. The animals, including man, cannot convert more than a limited amount of food per individual into energy, and that too not without considerable waste. Not only is the animal power plant quite inefficient, but it has to be stoked and fed all the time, whether any energy is utilised or not. You all know the low efficiency of coal and oil fuel. Hydro-electricity is better, but limited by lack of flexibility, and restriction to certain favourable localities.

What can humanity do with atomic energy? We must distinguish between what is now technically possible and what might theoretically be achieved in the very distant future. The most that has actually been done is to break down uranium nuclei, and to use the energy liberated. Other atomic nuclei can be broken down, but generally the process eats up more energy than it liberates. You know that this process has been misused. The atomic age arrived with a bang at Hiroshima and Nagasaki, in the form of a most deadly bomb. Its main use since then has been as a military and political weapon in the cold war, with which certain powers have tried to cow their opponents. The sun gets most of its energy from fusion. Four nuclei of hydrogen are squeezed together under immense heat and pressure to form one of helium. A certain amount of mass left over in the process is converted directly into energy, by Einstein's law. This has been done on earth in the hydrogen bomb. No materials known on earth can withstand the temperatures of fusion energy. If the available uranium were properly shared, we could convert many deserts into veritable gardens, industrialise the densest Amazon jungles, and free mankind from the worst forms of drudgery. This is no longer a technical problem, but a social one. A few pounds (about 8) of uranium sufficed to run a great submarine for seventy days. Automatic power plants could in theory be built which could be refuelled by air once every few months. Half a dozen trained men could run them. These plants could be located in any part of the world, without railways, waterways, or even road communication. But is the world prepared for this? The main question that most of you will ask is: What is the investment value of atomic energy? If the preliminary research and refining is to be done, there is virtually no investment value for the private sector. The whole affair is fantastically costly. Those who say that atomic energy can compete with thermal or hydro-power, carefully omit to mention the fact that the preliminary costs have always been written off to someone else's account, usually that of some government. Only in some socialist countries, where uranium is relatively plentiful, and new lands have to be opened up, is it possible to utilise atomic energy properly. Even there, military considerations play a considerable part, because of the cold war.

It is true that the known resources of radioactive material in the world exceed those known for coal. But the cost of uranium is artificially high. Then there is also the question of by-products. Animal by-products are good fertilisers; the skins and meat can also be used. For human beings, the by-products are taken care of by a good sewage system and the dead bodies by funerals. In industrial countries, the average temperature over cities (e.g. London) goes up by a couple of degrees Fahrenheit due to the use of coal. There is also the smoke, acid deposits that corrode buildings, carbon monoxide poisoning of the air by petrol fumes, and smog. These are trifling in comparison with the waste products of atomic power plants. The pile has to be very heavily shielded to screen harmful radiation. No one knows where to put the radioactive wastes from uranium piles. Every possible mine or pit is being rapidly filled up in the USA; the sea is unsafe, the rivers even more so. This is best brought out by the effects of atom-bomb tests. The fallout is found all over the world. The Bikini tests made grass in California radioactive and poisoned fish that would otherwise have fed Japanese a few thousand miles away. Excessive doses of radioactivity always cause serious changes in all living organisms. Some of these changes lie in the mechanism that enables the organism to breed. Most of these hereditary changes are lethal; that is, they kill the organisms born in the next generation. The Japanese have followed up persons exposed to atomic radiation at Hiroshima. Many of the children born to women who have been so exposed can hardly be called human; but they do not live to grow up. The real danger lies in the minute genetic change that does not show itself for some generations. It is known from experiments on smaller animals that these changes, when fully developed, may lead to incurable mental derangement within a few generations. By the time we know what the effect on mankind is going to be, it will be far too late to do anything about it. The changes will have been bred into millions of human beings of that generation and remain thereafter. This is not a disease, or an infection that I am talking about, but hereditary insanity, physical degeneracy, and worse. The only cure is to stop all atomic tests immediately, and to take great care that the waste products of atomic power stations for peaceful purposes will be safely isolated. The advanced countries have quietly reduced their atomic power programs. The prestige of having atomic power stations does not compensate the extra expenditure or the extra danger involved.

Where does that leave us in India? We do need every available source of power quickly. Can we utilise atomic power for national progress? This question has already been answered in the affirmative by the high command. The papers inform us that another hundred crores or more are to be devoted to this purpose, beyond undisclosed millions already spent. It was announced in August 1956 that India had joined the ranks of the atomic-energy producing countries. Actually, we were not then producing any atomic power. Though a second reactor costing another ten crores of rupees has gone into operation, and the staff has reached over two thousand highly trained graduates, we still produce no utilisable atomic power. The setting up of atomic power stations in other countries is now quite easy. Even China has one giving 7000 kilowatts since last year, and may build more. The USA, UK, USSR, France, Canada and some other countries could build one or more for us – if we are willing to pay the cost. The question is whether this cost is worthwhile.

I do not propose to answer this question, because all of you here are intelligent to work out the answer for yourselves. But I do wish to point out that the main work in producing atomic energy has already been done without cost to India by a permanent source, which has only to be utilised properly. This generous source is the sun, which goes on pouring its blasting rays into every tropical country, at an uncomfortable rate. Can solar energy be used directly?

The answer is yes. The USA, Russia or England, for example do not receive so much direct solar radiation as India. There is no reason why we should ape them in all things, including the development of atomic energy at a fantastic cost with low-grade Indian uranium. On an average day, every hundred square metres (1100 square feet) of area will receive about 600-kilowatt hours of heat. This comes to over

160 pounds of high-grade coal, or more than 16 gallons of petrol, in energy equivalent. If it could all be utilised at 100% efficiency, we could evaporate some 240 gallons of water per day. At present, the best known efficiency of utilisation is by solar batteries, which are between 11% and 15% efficient. The Americans are already using such batteries to boost telephone currents in long-distance lines. If I could use such batteries on my own bungalow roof, it means 7 kilowatts for every hour of average sunshine, say 60-kilowatt hours per day. This would give my family enough power for all cooking, lights, hot water, gadgets (vacuum cleaner, fridge), air-conditioning, and still leave enough for an electric automobile run on storage batteries. The Russians produce enough steam power from solar energy to supply all the needs of a modern town of over 15,000 inhabitants in the southern USSR. Even as early as 1876, a 2.5-horsepower steam pump was run on solar heat in Bombay. A striking instance of the immense reach of solar power comes from the space-satellites, which send their information to earth by radio transmitters that run on solar batteries. The best of them continued to communicate with our globe from well over 20 million miles away.

It seems to me that research on the utilisation of solar radiation, where the fuel costs nothing at all, would be of immense benefit to India, whether or not atomic energy is used. But by research is not meant the writing of a few papers, sending favoured delegates to international conferences and pocketing of considerable research grants by those who can persuade complaisant politicians to sanction crores of the taxpayers' money. Our research has to be translated into use. The catch in solar energy is its storage. The current you may want at night can be produced irregularly in the daytime. This is not an insoluble difficulty. Quite efficient forms of storage batteries are known. It is possible to combine several uses with mechanical storage. For example, water could be pumped up into 50-foot village towers during sunlight hours, and then allowed to run out for irrigation, or home use, through low-pressure turbines that generate electricity whenever wanted. This is not very efficient at the second stage, but the main purpose of augmenting our poor water supply will have been efficiently served, village-by-village.

The most important advantage of solar energy would be decentralisation. To electrify India with a complete national grid would be difficult, considering our peculiar distribution of hydropower and thermal resources. With solar energy, you can supply power locally, with or without a grid. Solar power would be the best available source of energy for dispersed small industry and local use in India. If you really mean to have socialism in any form, without the stifling effects of bureaucracy and heavy initial investment, there is no other source so efficient. Take the simple problem of reforestation, which alone can change India's agriculture, preserve her rapidly eroding soil, and increase production. This problem is insoluble unless people have cheap fuel for cooking, so that they need not cut down trees. The solar cooker if it worked, would have been the answer. We know that the cooker produced some years ago with such fanfare and self-congratulation is useless. Even a schoolboy should have known that the pot at the focus of the solar cooker, being nickelled and polished, would reflect away most of the heat. But our foremost physicists and research workers who rushed to claim personal credit and publicity did not realise this. That is the result of paper research and research for advertisement. If we get over this fundamental hurdle, we have the real cost-free source of atomic power, the sun, at our disposal for more than eight months of the year.

Solar energy is not something that any villager can convert for use with his own unaided efforts, at a negligible personal expenditure, charkha style. It means good science and first-rate technology whose results must be made available to the individual user. The solar water heater is the simplest to manufacture: a black absorbing grid like an automobile radiator and an insulated storage-tank. No moving parts are involved. The water can be delivered much hotter than needed for a bath, but below the boiling point. Such heaters are already used successfully in Israel and elsewhere, and would save a great deal of fuel by themselves in the Indian household. For the steam engine, it is necessary to concentrate the sun's rays, usually by a light silvered concave reflector which moves with the sun. These are also quite practicable and in use. Direct conversion of sunlight into electricity is familiar to many of us as the photoelectric cell, and the photometer used for correct exposure. These are very simple and efficient to use, but cost more money to make. The technique has now been simplified and the cost reduced by careful study of semiconductors. The most effective solar battery of which I have any knowledge is based upon silicon-zinc crystals. Their production, too, is commercially successful, but needs still more research–which continues uninterrupted in other countries. The Chinese use semi-conductors directly to produce enough electricity even from the waste heat of an ordinary kerosene lamp to run a radio set; their appliances are on the international market now.

What India could use best in this way still remains to be determined. The principle involved in the use of atomic energy produced by the sun as against that from atomic piles is parallel to that between small and large dams for irrigation. The large dam is very impressive to look at, but its construction and use mean heavy expenditure in one locality, and bureaucratic administration. The small bunding operation can be done with local labour, stops erosion of the soil, and can be fitted into any corner of the country where there is some rainfall. It solves two fundamental problems: how to keep the rain-water from flowing off rapidly into the sea, unused; and how to encourage local initiative while giving direct economic gain to the small producer. The great dams certainly have their uses, but no planners should neglect proper emphasis upon effective construction of the dispersed small dams. What is involved is not merely agriculture and manufacture, but a direct road to socialism.

Every notable advance in man's control over new sources of energy has been hampered by outworn superstition or obsolete social forms. Fire is regarded today as a convenient tool it the service of humanity. Primitive man thought it necessary to worship fire as a god. Agni received human and animal sacrifice; vestal virgins might be dedicated to his service. Is it less miserable a superstition that calls for the sacrifice of millions of men and animals, living or as yet unborn, to atomic tests and radioactive fallout? It seemed inevitable to Victorian England that dreadful industrial slums should accompany the first large scale use of the steam engine; it also seemed necessary to conquer many colonies for supply of raw materials and as market for the finished goods of the factories that the steam engine first made possible.

We claim to know better now. If so, has the time not come to change society so that the new discoveries will serve the needs of all mankind rather than the perverted greed of the few? Then, and only then, will it be possible to determine how much effort should be spent relatively on the development of the various sources of energy.

CHAPTER 4

Adventure into the Unknown

1. Why Science?

The question 'Why solve problems?' is psychological. It is as necessary for some as breathing. Why scientific problems, not theology, or literary effort, or some form of artistic expression? Many practising scientists never work out the answer consciously. Those lands where the leading intellectuals speculated exclusively upon religious philosophy and theology remained ignorant, backward and were progressively enslaved (like India) in spite of a millennial culture. No advance was possible out of this decay without modern techniques of production, towards which the intellectuals' main contribution was through science. There is a deeper relationship: Science is the cognition of necessity ; freedom is the recognition of necessity. By finding out why a certain thing happens, we turn it to our advantage rather than be ruled helplessly by the event. Science is also the history of science. What is essential is absorbed into the general body of human knowledge, to become technique. No scientist doubts Newton's towering achievement; virtually no scientist ever reads Newton in the original. A good undergraduate commands decidedly more physics and mathematics than was known to Newton, but which could not have developed without Newton's researches. This cumulative effect links science to the technology of mechanised production (where machine saves immense labour by accumulating previous labour) to give science its matchless social power in contrast to art and literature with their direct personal appeal. Archimedes, Newton and Gauss form a chain wherein each link is connected in some way to the preceding; the discoveries of the latter would not have been possible without the earlier. Shakespeare does not imply the pre-existence of Æschylus or of Kalidasa; each of these three has an independent status. For that very reason, drama has advanced far less from the Greeks to the present day than has mathematics or science in general. Even the anonymous statues of Egypt and Greece or the first Chinese bronzes show a command of technique, material and of art forms that make them masterpieces ; but the art is not linked to production as such, hence not cumulative. The artist survives to the extent that his name remains attached to some work that people of later ages can appreciate. The scientist, even when his name be forgotten, or his work buried under the wrong tombstone, has only to make some original contribution, however small, to be able to feel with more truth than the poet, "I shall not wholly die; The greater part of me will escape Libitina" . The most bitter theological questions were argued out with the sword; for science, we have the pragmatic test, experiment, which is more civilised except when some well-paid pseudo-scientist wishes to 'experiment' with thermo-nuclear weapons or bacterial warfare.

2. Natural Philosophy

It was obligatory for me to learn several European languages in school and college in the USA. The libraries were the best in the world for accessibility and range of books. Alexander von Humboldt's Cosmos surveyed the whole universe known to the middle of the nineteenth century, from the earth to those mysterious prawn-shaped figures visible through powerful telescopes, the spiral nebulae. The Einstein theory, arousing passions of theological intensity, had just been regarded as proved, and offered new insight into the structure of space, time and matter. Innumerable outlines made it easy to learn something about every branch of science. Freud had taught men to take an honest look at their own minds. H.G. Wells showed in his *Outline of History* how much the professional annalistic historian had to learn, though Spengler's *Untergang des Abendlandes* made it extremely unlikely that the historian would learn it. The inspiring lives of Pasteur and Claude Bernard proved that man could gain new freedom from disease through the laboratory; the deadliest poison became a tool for the saving of life through investigation of the body's functions. Such were the real *ṛṣi*s and *bodhisattva*s of modern times, the sages whose scientific achievement added to man's stature. This contrasted with the supposed inner perfection of mythical Indian sages, expressed in incomprehensible language and fantastically interpreted by commentators. The ability to replace incomprehensible Sanskrit words by still longer and equally meaningless English terms can make a prosperous career. It cannot produce an Albert Schweitzer, whose magnificent study *Von Reimarus zu Wrede*, analysis of Bach's music and record as medical missionary at Lambarene were impressive even in my irreverent undergraduate years.

Engineering is based upon physics and chemistry, which are qualified as 'exact sciences' precisely because they admit a mathematical basis. Mathematics unlocked the door to the atom and to the movement of celestial bodies equally well. Aptitude granted, mathematical research needed the least financial resources of any science. Mathematical results possess a clarity and give an intellectual satisfaction above all others. They have absolute validity in their own domain, due to the rigorous logical process involved, independent of experimental verification upon which applications to the exact sciences must depend. This was the very language of nature, *scientiarum clavis et porta* as Roger Bacon put it. Its supreme, transcendental, aesthetic fascination can only be experienced, never explained.

Unfortunately, not every kind of mathematics unlocks every door to nature's secrets. For some twenty years, my main work lay in tensor analysis and path-geometry (my own term). The structure of space-time had been analysed by the measurement of 'distance' in space and time; I showed that it could be done without distance, merely by the racks that explored the 'space', even when the concept of 'space' was generalised beyond physical recognition. In 1949, Einstein pointed out to me during one of several long and highly involved private technical discussions that certain beautifully formulated theories of his would mean that the whole universe consisted of no more than two charged particles. Then he added with a rueful smile, 'Perhaps I have been working on the wrong lines, and nature does not obey differential equations after all'. If a scientist of his rank could face the possibility that his entire lifework might have to be discarded, why insist that the theorems whose inner beauty brought me so much pleasure after heavy toil must be of profound significance in natural philosophy? Fashions change quickly in physics where theory is so rapidly outstripped by experiment. It seemed and still seems to me that non-associative linear algebras and Markov chains would remove many of the physicists' theoretical difficulties; the experimenters are satisfied with abandoning the principle of parity. The 'red shift' of distant stars will perhaps be explained one day as due to the absorption of energy when light travels at cosmic distances through extremely tenuous matter, rather than evidence for an expanding universe. Such speculations are of no use unless they tally in mathematical detail with observed data.

3. Chance and Certainty

Borderline phenomena of classical physics illustrate the in exhaustibility of the properties of matter. Ice, according to the textbooks, melts and water freezes at zero degrees Centigrade. But when carefully purified samples of water are slowly cooled and the ice slowly melted again, a considerable gap is found between the melting and freezing points. Fundamental particles that make-up the atom and its nucleus show another type of aberrant behaviour. An electron can cross a potential barrier, as if a stone were of itself to roll uphill against gravity, and down the other side. Even the observation of isolated particles becomes difficult, for the very act of observation means some interaction and effect upon the observable. The certainty of classical physics develops only when many fundamental particles are organised into higher units with clear patterns. In the same way, individual molecules of water may move in any direction with almost any speed, but the river as a whole shows directed motion in spite of eddies. So also for aggregates of living matter. In human society, the net behaviour of the group smooths out the vagaries of individual action.

The mathematical analysis best suited for handling such aggregates is the theory of probability. Variation is as important a characteristic of the collective as the mean value. Prediction can only be made within a certain probability, which sounds like the language of the race course. But when the chances of a mistake amount to one in a million, most people take the effect as certain. The level of significance desired may be a personal matter. For example, there is a chance of a letter being lost in the mail; whether or not we register or insure it depends upon our estimate of the risk involved and the expectation of loss. Thus, modern statistical method can be an excellent guide to action. It extends the assurance of exact science to biological and social sciences. Though no man can say when death will come to him, as it certainly must, it is fairly easy to predict within a reasonable margin of error about how many men out of a large group will die after a set number of years. That is why life insurance manages to be a highly paying business, without recourse to astrology. It is further possible to say how occupation and living conditions affect longevity. The man who has to work in a lead mine (without special protection) has his expectation of life reduced by a predictable number of years, more surely than if he were shot at by lead bullets on the battlefield.

Deductions based upon probability differ radically from those of pure mathematics. Conclusions cannot be 'true or false' without qualification, when the variation inherent in the trials is assessed. The standard method is to set up a 'null hypothesis', take the observed results as due to purely random independent variation. The theory suitably applied (and the application needs profound grasp) then gives one of two conclusions : that the numerical observations (if relevant) are compatible with the hypothesis; or not. But either conclusion would be true only with a certain calculable probability, which tells us about how often we would go wrong in action. The trick is to set up the experiment in such a way that the desired action may be taken if the null hypothesis is contradicted; for, incompatibility implies falsehood whereas compatibility need not imply truth.

This may lead to difficulties when the experimenter's will to believe is stronger than his common sense. Parapsychologists test *ESP*, 'extra-sensory perception' (such as telepathy) by having two people match cards at a distance. The effect is so faint and irregular as to call for delicate statistical tests, which show that the chances are very small, for random matching, wherefore the parapsychologists claim victory. Unfortunately, my own experiments showed that the kind of shuffling practised for *ESP* is inefficient when judged by the same kind of statistics that is applied to card matching. Cards originally next to each other tend too often to stay together. Claims of *ESP* would be more convincing if one produced supplementary evidence (say matching encephalograms for sender and receiver) for a physical mechanism of transmission. Some regard the effect as beyond normal sensation, transcendental, not accessible to material analysis. In that case, laboratory tests and the statistical 'proof' become mere ritual.[1]

One of my theoretical papers deals with probability and statistics in infinitely many dimensions. There has been no effective use, because we could not get or make the special electronic calculating machine needed to translate this theory into practice. On the other hand, a brief note on genetics was unexpectedly successful. Professional geneticists use it for all kinds of investigations, such as heredity in house mice. It seems to have given a new lease of life to genetical theories which I, personally, should like to see revised. I am accused at times of not appreciating my own formula. It would have been pleasant to see the formula applied to the increase of food production but the pure scientists of the country which grows the world's greatest food surpluses and suppresses or destroys

1 All the well-designed experiments in parapsychology have used random procedures for target selection, and the statistics used in ESP research were approved by the American Statistical Institute as early as in the 1930's.-K. R. Rao.

them to keep grain prices high in a hungry world sneer at 'clever gardening'. There is some difference of opinion here as regards the proper relation of theory to practice.

4. Ancient Indian Culture

To teach myself statistics, I decided to take up some practical problems from the very beginning. One such was the study of examination marks of students. It turned out that even the easiest of examinations in India (the first-year college examination) was based on a standard that differed from that of the instruction, if in twenty-five years no student of the 90 per cent or more that passed could score more than 82 per cent overall while the professors who taught and examined had scored much less in their own time. Improvement of the system (whether in examination or instruction) was out of the question in a country where the teaching profession is the wastebasket of all 'white-clothes' occupations and the medium of higher instruction still remains a foreign language.

A more fruitful problem was the statistical study of punch-marked coins. It turned out that the apparently crude bits of 'shroff-marked' silver were coins carefully weighed as modern machine-minted rupees. The effect of circulation on any metal currency is obviously to decrease the average weight in proportion to the time and to increase the variation in weight. This is the mark any society leaves upon its coinage, just by use. The theory of this 'homogeneous random process' is well known, but its application meant the careful weighing, one at a time, of over 7,000 modern coins as control. Numismatics becomes a science rather than a branch of epigraphy and archaeology. The main groups of punch-marked coins in the larger Taxila Hoard could be arranged in definite chronological order, the oldest groups being the lightest in average weight. There seems to have been a fairly regular pre-Mauryan system of checking silver coins.

Arranging coin-groups in order of time led naturally to the question: who struck these coins? The hoard was deposited a few years after Alexander's death : but who left the marks on the coins? The shockingly discordant written sources (*Purāṇas*, Buddhist and Jain records) often give different names for the same king. Study of the records meant knowledge of Sanskrit, of which I had absorbed a little through the pores. Other preoccupations made it impossible to learn the classical idiom like any other beginner. So, the same method was adopted as for study of statistics: to take up a specific work, of which the simplest was Bhartrhari's epigrams (*subhāṣitas*). The supposed philosophy of Bhartrhari, as glorified by commentators, was at variance with his poetry of frustration and escape. By pointing this out in an essay which caused every god-fearing Sanskritist to shudder, I fell into Indology, as it were, through the roof.

There was one defect in the essay, in that the existence and the text of Bhartrhari were both rather uncertain. This meant text criticism, which ought to have been completed in a few months, as the entire work supposedly contains no more than 300 stanzas. Study of about 400 manuscripts yielded numerous versions with characteristically different stanzas, as well as divergent readings in the common verses. Two and a half years of steady collation work showed that I should never have undertaken such a task: but abandoning it then would mean complete loss of the heavy labour, which could yield nothing to whoever came after me. It took five years to edit Bhartrhari, but even the critics who dislike the editor or his philosophy maintain that the result is a landmark in text criticism. Different methods were needed to edit (with a very able collaborator) the oldest known anthology of classical Sanskrit verse, composed about A. D. 1100 under the Pāla dynasty. The main sources were atrocious photographs of a palm-leaf manuscript in Tibet, and of a most corrupt paper manuscript in Nepal. My judgment of the class character of Sanskrit literature has not become less harsh, but I can at least claim to have rescued over fifty poets from the total oblivion to which lovers of Sanskrit had consigned them.

All this gave a certain grasp of Sanskrit, but hardly of ancient Indian history; the necessary documents simply did not exist. My countrymen eked out doubtful sources with an exuberant imagination and what L. Renou has called 'logique imperturbable'. One reads of the revival of Nationalism and Hinduism under Chandragupta II, of whom nothing is known with certainty. Indian nationalism is a phenomenon of the bourgeois age, not to be imagined before the development of provincial languages (long after the Guptas) under distinct common markets. Our present-day clashes between linguistic groups are an index to the development of local bourgeoisies in the various states. Hinduism came into existence after Mohammedan invasion. Clearly, one of two positions had to be taken. Either India has no history at all, or some better definition of history was needed. The latter I derived from the study of Karl Marx, who himself expressed the former view. History is the development in chronological order of successive changes in the means and relations of production. Thus slavery in the Graeco-Roman sense was replaced by the caste system in India only because commodity production was at a lower level. Indian history has to be written without the episodes that fill the history books of other countries. But what were the relevant sources? Granted that the plough is more important than a dynasty, when and where was the tool first introduced? What class took the surplus produced thereby? Archaeology provided some data, but I could get a great deal more from the peasants. Field work in philology and social anthropology had to be combined with archaeology in the field as distinguished from the site archaeology of a 'dig'. Our villagers, low caste nomads, and tribal minorities live at a more primitive stage than city people or the brahmins who wrote the *purāṇas*. Their cults, when not masked by brahmin identification with Sanskritised deities, go back to prehistory like the stone axes used in Roman sacrifices. Tracing a local god through village tradition gives a priceless clue to ancient migrations, primitive tracks, early trade routes and the merger of cattle breeding tribesmen with food gatherers which led to firm agricultural settlement. The technique of observation has to be developed afresh for every province in India. The conclusions published as *An Introduction to the Study of Indian History* had a mixed reception because of the reference to Marx, which automatically classifies them as dangerous political agitation in the eyes of many, while official Marxists look with suspicion upon the work of an outsider.

Field investigation continues to give new and useful results. Experts say glumly that my collection of microliths is unique not only in range of sites but in containing pierced specimens. A totally unsuspected megalithic culture came to light this year. It fell to my lot to discover, read and publish a Brāhmi inscription at Kārle caves, which had passed unnoticed though in plain sight of the 50,000 people who visit the place every year. The suggestion for using the Māḷsheṭ Pass should give Maharashtra a badly needed key road from Bombay to Ahmadnagar, and save a few million rupees though the funicular railway down Nāneghāṭ would have been more spectacular.

5. Social Aspects

The greatest obstacles to research in any backward, underdeveloped country are those needlessly created by the scientist's or scholar's colleagues and fellow citizens. The meretricious ability to please the right people, an attractive pose, glib charlatanism and a clever press agent are indispensable. Mere scientific ability is at a discount. The Byzantine emperor Nikephoros Phokas assured himself of ample notice from superficial observers, at someone else's expense by setting up in his own name at a strategic site in the Roman Forum, a column pilfered from some grandiose temple. Many eminent intellectuals have mastered this technique in India.

The deep question is not what floats to the top of a stagnant class but of fundamental relationship between the great discoverers and their social environment. Conservatives take history as the personal achievement of great men, especially the history of science. The Marxist assertion is that the great man is he who finds some way to fulfil a deep though perhaps unstated social need of his times. Thus, B. Hessen explained Newton's work in terms of the technical and economic necessities of his class, time and place. The thesis was successful enough to be noticed and contested by a distinguished authority on 17th century European history, Sir George Clark. Clark's knowledge of the sources is unquestionably greater than Hessen's, but the refutation manages to overreach the argument. According to Clark, the scientific movement (of the 17th century) was set going by 'six interpenetrating but independent impulses' from outside and 'some of its results percolated down into practice and were applied'. The external impulses were 'from economic life, from war, from medicine, from the arts, and from religion. What is left then of the independence of science?' The sixth impulse was from the 'disinterested desire to know'. So far as I know, all six impulses applied from the very earliest civilizations of Mesopotamia, Egypt, China and probably the Indus Valley, without producing what we recognise as 'science' from, say, the time of Galileo. What was the missing ingredient, if not the rise of the proto-bourgeoisie in Europe? No Marxist would claim that science can be independent of the social system within which the scientist must function.

Much the same treatment may be given to literature. Disregarding oversimplification, can one say that Shakespeare's plays manifest the rise of the Elizabethan proto-bourgeoisie, when the said dramas are full of kings, lords and princes? The answer is yes. Compare *Hamlet* or *Richard the Third* with the leading characters in *Beowulf* or the *Chanson de Roland.* The fattest Shakespearean parts like Shylock and Falstaff are difficult to visualise in any feudal literature. The characters in those plays have a 'modern' psychology, which accounts for their appeal to the succeeding bourgeoisie, and hence for the survival value of the dramas. Troilus and Cressida are not feudal characters any more than they are Homeric; Newton's Latin prose and archaic geometrical proofs in the *Principia* make that work unreadable, but do not make it Roman or Greek science.

It would take a whole book to develop this thesis for India's trifling successes and considerable failure in modern science. In what follows, only the most obvious defects in applying science to major Indian problems are considered, without discussion of the extent to which this accounts for the lack of really great scientists in India.

India, the experts tell us, is over-populated and will remain poor unless birth control and population planning is introduced. But surely, overpopulation can only be with respect to the available food supply. Availability depends upon production, transport, and the system of distribution. What is the total amount of food produced? We have theological quarrels between two schools of statisticians, but no reliable estimate of how much is actually grown and what proportion thereof escapes vermin – including middlemen and profiteers – to reach the consumer. If shopkeepers can and do raise prices without effective control, what does a rise in the national income mean? Is the scarcity of grain or of purchasing power? A great deal is said about superstitious common people who must be educated before birth control becomes effective. The superstition which makes the poor long for children has a solid economic foundation. Children are the sole means of support for those among the common people who manage to reach helpless old age. The futility of numerical 'planning' of the population, when nothing is done to ensure that even the able-bodied have a decent level of subsistence, is obvious to anyone but a born expert. Convince the people that even the childless will be fed and looked after when unable to fend for themselves and birth control will become popular.

Let me give examples of scientific effort which could easily have been turned to better account. Considerable funds will be devoted during the Third Plan to research on the uses of bagasse (sugarcane pulp). At present, it is used as fuel and the ashes as fertilizer, whereas paper and many other things could be made from it. But are the other uses (quite well known) the best in the present state of Indian economy? The extra money to be spent on fuel, not to speak of difficulties in getting fuel, would increase the already high cost of sugar manufacture; new factories for by-products mean considerable foreign exchange for the machinery, and for the 'experts'. However, if the bagasse is fermented in closed vats, the gas given off can be burned, so that the fuel value is not reduced. The sludge makes excellent fertilizer, which saves money on chemical fertilizers and improves the soil. The scheme (not mine, but due to Hungarian scientists) has apparently been pushed into the background. Again, the proper height of a dam is important in order to reduce the outlay to a minimum, without the risk of running dry more than (say) once in twenty years. The problem is statistical, based upon the rainfall and runoff data where both exist. The principles I suggested were adopted by the Planning Commission, though not as emanating from me. Neither the engineers nor the Planning Commission, would consider a more important suggestion, namely, that many cheap small dams should be located by plan and built from local materials with local labour. Monsoon water would be conserved and two or three crops raised annually on good soil that now yields only one. The real obstacle is not ignorance of technique but private ownership of land and lack of co-operation among the owners.

This country needs every form of power available, but is too poor to throw money away on costly fads like atomic energy merely because they look ultra-modern. A really paying development will be of solar energy, neglected by the advanced countries because they have not so much sunlight as the tropics. Our problem lies deeper than power production. The reforestation, indispensable for good agriculture, will not be possible without fuel to replace firewood and charcoal. Coal mining does not suffice even for industry; fuel oil has to be imported. A good solar cooker would be the answer. Such cookers exist and have been used abroad. The one produced in India was hopelessly inefficient (in spite of the many Indian physicists of international reputation). Neatly timed publicity and a fake demonstration made the gullible public buy just enough useless 'cookers' for a quick profit to the manufacturer. A flimsy 'Indian Report' on the effects of atomic radiation shows our low moral and scientific calibre by ignoring the extensive data compiled since 1945 in the one country which has had the most painful experience of atomic radiation applied to human beings – Japan. The real danger is not death, which is a release for most Indians, but genetic damage to all humanity. We know what radiation does to heredity in the ephemeral banana-fly *Drosophila melanogaster*. A good deal was found out in the U.S.A. about what happens to laboratory mice. What little has been released for publication is enough to terrify. Man is as much more complicated than a mouse as the mouse than the fruit-fly. Humans take a proportionately longer time to breed and to reach maturity, giving fuller scope for genetic derangements to develop. It may take some twenty generations to find out just what these derangements amount to. By then they will have been bred into many millions of human beings, not as a disease but incurably as a set of hereditary characters. Mankind cannot afford to gamble with its own future in this way, whether that future lies in the hands of communists or not. Atomic war and the testing of nuclear weapons must stop. These views on nuclear war are now fashionable enough to be safely expressed.

6. Epilogue

A mathematician must earn that designation by enriching mathematics with original theorems of basic importance. Einstein, for all the stimulus his ideas gave to contemporary differential geometry, was not, and never regarded himself as a mathematician. So, my excursions into statistics, Indology, archaeology and the rest are irrelevant unless some real mathematics emerged at the end. Alternatively, is there something wrong in the philosophy that asserts the unity of theory and practice?

Mathematics is no longer the by-product of a natural philosopher's investigations, as it had been from Pythagoras to Gauss. All sorts of mathematical technique exist today, fully developed long before the physicist feels the need for it. One should contrast G. H. Hardy's *Mathematician's Apology* (Cambridge, 1941) with L. Hogben's *Mathematics for the Million* (London, 1936). The former, though leader and virtually creator of the modern school of British mathematics, was indifferent to applications and the social context of mathematical discovery. Those were the aspects of mathematics of primary interest to the biologist Hogben, who thereby presented rather elementary mathematics in attractive popularisation. Hardy counted uselessness among the great assets of real mathematics; forgetting Archimedes's military engines, he blamed 'Hogben mathematics' for the senseless destruction of world wars. This was just before the manufacture of nuclear weapons by the 'Science has known Sin' group, in collaboration with outstanding mathematicians like J. von Neumann. If any important mathematics came out of the atomic and hydrogen bombs, the secret has been well kept.

The theory of numbers is the oldest branch of mathematics. Hogben mathematics would not exist without numbers, while Hardy and his associates devoted their best efforts to number-theory. Two outstanding problems here are : (1) Fermat's Last Theorem, which can be explained to a schoolboy in spite of its melodramatic title; (2) The Riemann Hypothesis, decidedly more recondite. Both have defeated the efforts of great mathematicians to prove or to disprove them. The Fermat theorem, if true, would lead to no new mathematics; proof of the Riemann conjecture would lay the very foundations of analytic number theory. These unsolved problems gave rise to a distressing possibility in mathematical reasoning: was there a category of propositions 'neither (demonstrably) true nor false'?

Riemann's conjecture has to do with the distribution of primes, which are those integers (like 257) not divisible by any smaller number except unity. Every whole number can be expressed in just one way as the product of primes, hence their importance. There are infinitely many primes. A given integer is either a prime or not, with no question of probability; yet the occurrence of primes among the integers is highly irregular, without a pattern. Given a specific prime, it is always possible to find the next by hard work, but not by formula. This parallels an experimental situation. Weights of coins of the same denomination fluctuate so much that I could never predict what the next coin would show on delicate balances. However, if there was a next coin, its weight could always be recorded as one more figure of a series. Enough such figures outlined a curve for the distribution of weights. The series of weights formed a *sample* from a population assumed subject to probability laws. Could something of the sort not be proved for the primes? It was necessary to change the scale, because primes occur with less and less frequency (on the whole) as the integers grow larger. The change gave a fixed *average* number of primes per interval of any constant length on the changed scale. Still, the number varied unpredictably from interval to interval. The number of primes per interval was then shown by me to follow a simple though unsuspected probability law, the Poisson distribution. This describes many experimental samples such as the number of cosmic rays per second, of bacteria in thin cultures, of calls in a telephone exchange. Previous failures in prime number theory resulted from the attempt to fit an exact description to an infinite set of infinite random samples.

Every competent judge who saw only this radically new basic result intuitively felt that it was correct as well as of fundamental importance. Unfortunately, the Riemann hypothesis followed as a simple consequence. Could a problem over which the world's greatest mathematicians had come to grief for over a century be thus casually solved in the jungles of India? Psychologically, it seemed much more probable that the interloper was just another 'circle-squarer'. Mathematics may be a cold, impersonal science of pure thought; the mathematician can be thoughtless, heatedly acrid, even rabid, over what he dislikes. Let me admit at once that I made every sort of mistake in the first presentation. There is no excuse for this, though there were strong reasons: I had to fight for my results over three long years between waves of agony from chronic arthritis, against massive daily doses of aspirin, splitting headaches, fever, lack of assistance and steady disparagement. It was much more difficult to discover good mathematicians who were able to see the main point of the proof than it had been to make the original mathematical discovery. How much of this is due to my own disagreeable personality and what part to the spirit of a tight medieval guild that rules mathematical circles in certain countries with an 'affluent society' need not be considered here. There is surely a great deal to be said for the notion that the success of science is fundamentally related to the particular form of society.

www.ingramcontent.com/pod-product-compliance
Ingram Content Group UK Ltd.
Pitfield, Milton Keynes, MK11 3LW, UK
UKHW022006190726
13853UKWH00004B/1767